AF366884

## AUTHOR

**Paolo Crippa** (23 April 1978) has cultivated his passion for Italian history since high school. His research interests are focused mainly in the field of military history and in particular on italian armored units from the 30s until the end of World War II. In 2006 he published his first volume, *"I Reparti Corazzati della Repubblica Sociale Italiana 1943/1945"*, the first organic research carried out and published in Italy on the subject. In 2007 he published *"Duecento Volti della R.S.I."* and in 2011 *" Un anno con il 27° Reggimento Artiglieria Legnano"*. He regularly contributes to several journals: Milites, New Historica, SGM - World War II, Batailes & Blindes, Armoured Vehicles and history of the twentieth century, Mezzi Corazzati, both as an author, or in collaboration with other researchers. He published with the editor Mattioli 1885 in 2014 *"Italy 43 – 45 – Civil War improvised AFV's"* (2014), *"Italian AFV's of the Civil War 1943 - 1945"* (2015) and *"Italy 43 – 45 – AFV's and MV's of co-belligerent units"* (2018).

## PUBLISHING'S NOTES

None of unpublished images or text of our book may be reproduced in any format without the expressed written permission of Luca Cristini Editore (already Soldiershop.com) when not indicate as marked with license creative commons 3.0 or 4.0. Luca Cristini Editore has made every reasonable effort to locate, contact and acknowledge rights holders and to correctly apply terms and conditions to Content.

Every effort has been made to trace the copyright of all the photographs. If there are unintentional omissions, please contact the publisher in writing at: info@soldiershop.com, who will correct all subsequent editions.

Our trademark: Luca Cristini Editore©, and the names of our series & brand: Soldiershop, Witness to war, Museum book, Bookmoon, Soldiers&Weapons, Battlefield, War in colour, Historical Biographies, Darwin's view, Fabula, Altrastoria, Italia Storica Ebook, Witness To History, Soldiers, Weapons & Uniforms, Storia etc. are herein © by Luca Cristini Editore.

## LICENSES COMMONS

This book may utilize part of material marked with license creative commons 3.0 or 4.0 (CC BY 4.0), (CC BY-ND 4.0), (CC BY-SA 4.0) or (CC0 1.0). We give appropriate attribution credit and indicate if change were made in the acknowledgments field. Our WTW books series utilize only fonts licensed under the SIL Open Font License or other free use license.

For a complete list of Soldiershop titles please contact Luca Cristini Editore on our website: www.soldiershop.com or www.cristinieditore.com. E-mail: info@soldiershop.com

Title: **THE ARMORED UNITS OF THE ROYAL ARMY AND THE ARMISTICE VOL. 1** Code.: WTW-023 EN
by Paolo Crippa  ISBN code: 978-88-93277303  First edition March 2021
Text in English Nr. of images: 112  Layout: 177,8x254mm  Cover & Art Design: Luca S. Cristini

**WITNESS TO WAR (SOLDIERSHOP)** is a trademark of Luca Cristini Editore, via Orio, 35/4 - 24050 Zanica (BG) ITALY.

**WITNESS TO WAR**

# THE ARMORED UNITS OF THE ROYAL ARMY AND THE ARMISTICE VOL. 1

PHOTOS & IMAGES FROM WORLD WARTIME ARCHIVES

**PAOLO CRIPPA**

BOOKS TO COLLECT

# CONTENTS

▲ In Rome, after the clashes following the Armistice and the capitulation of the Italian armed forces, two agents of the P.A.I., armed with the M.A.B. machine gun with the characteristic folding bayonet, argue with one of their officers, while behind them German soldiers control a crossroads with a position armed with a 75mm anti-tank gun (B.A.).

# INTRODUCTION

When today we speak about "*September 8th*", we generally refer to the disastrous dissolution of the Armed Forces and of the Nation, due above all to the unfortunate way in which the majority of the Italian military became aware of it and to the abandonment in which the units in arms were left by the leadership, that should have instead guided them in that surreal and sudden transition of front. In those moments, the responses of entire units and individual soldiers were very different from each other: strong units dissolved, others decided to resist German attacks, others still opted to continue the war alongside the German armed forces. The Italian armored units, both Tankers and Cavalry, were scattered not only on the national territory, but also abroad: not even they were immune to the storm unleashed by the Armistice and even from these units the reactions to Badoglio's tragic announcement were the most disparate. Through an accurate analysis, in the pages of this book we will analyze how the armored units behaved in those tragic moments, in a synthesis that until now has never been proposed. The units that opposed the attacks brought by the Germans, although in need of armaments, fought for reasons of desperation, in a war that was now lost, and for a touch of military pride. For this reason, it is right to retrace the events of those days, to pay homage to the fallen and to all those who did their duty to the end.

This first volume deals, in a particular way, with the events that led to the loss of the Capital, where, on the eve of the Armistice, many units of Tankers and Armored Cavalry were located. As we will see, the German reaction to the change of front of the Kingdom of Italy was timely and particularly aggressive, since Hitler was furious for what he considered a real betrayal and created a climate of turmoil among the defenders of Rome. The Italians, who were actually superior to the attackers in means and men (and with such a superiority that they could have had reason with the Germanic forces) consequently faced the German attacks in an almost "brancaleonic" way. This, however, did not prevent entire armored units from sacrificing themselves in an extreme attempt to defend the Eternal City.

As always, I face every new research work with enthusiasm and with respect for the events (and above all the people, actors on the stage of History) of which I will speak. But to carry out any study, this is not enough, documents are not enough, but we need the contribution of many Friends who bring, each to a different extent, but all in an equally valuable way, their incredible help. I would like to mention, in random order, Lorenzo Tonioli, Luigi Manes, Antonio Tallillo and Ralph Ricco, who "hunted" for photographs from their archives, news, documents and books. I would also like to thank Colonel Maurizio Parri, who shared memories and photographs of his father Raffaello's experience as a young officer in the 4th Tankers Regiment in Rome. I cannot forget the late Nino Arena and Giorgio Pisanò, who generously opened their archives to me. And finally, a thank you to Fabio D'Inzeo, officer of the Cavalry, "gone ahead" in September 2020, for the many news he shared with me in long years of friendship. I dedicate this work to him, happy to have known him and to have had him as a Friend, sharing the passion for History and for Modelling: we spent many pleasant and unforgettable moments together. Thank you all!

The Author

▲ Italian soldiers photographed in Rome on July 26, 1943, the day after the arrest of Benito Mussolini (Manes).

# THE ARMISTICE AND THE ARMORED UNITS

**A**t the beginning of September 1943, the units of the Tankers and the Armored Cavalry of the Regio Esercito were dramatically divided, both on the national territory and outside the borders, in addition to being tried (in morale, in the staff and in the endowment of armored means) by 3 years of war, which, especially on the African front, had drained every offensive potential with a continuous dripping of crews and equipment.

There were 7 Depots for the Infantry Tanker units in the country:

- 1st Regiment Tanker Infantry (Vercelli):
    - o   Command
    - o   Depot XIII Tank Battalion
- 3° Tanker Infantry Regiment (Bologna):
    - o   Vittorio Emanuele II Lancers Regiment
    - o   15th Tank Company [1]
- 4th Regiment Tanker Infantry (Rome):
    - o   Mixed Tank Battalion (formerly called XI Battalion)
- 31st Tanker Infantry Regiment (Siena):
    - o   Command of the 31st Infantry Regiment
    - o   Command of 131st Infantry Regiment
    - o   XV Tank Battalion
    - o   XIX Tank Battalion
    - o   6th, 7th, 8th Company
- 32nd Regiment Tanker Infantry (Verona):
    - o   1st, 2nd, 3rd Company
    - o   1st Autonomous Company
    - o   XVIII Tank Battalion M
- 33rd Regiment Tanker Infantry (Parma):
    - o   4th Self-propelled Battery
    - o   5th Self-propelled Battery
    - o   CCCXXXIII Tank Complement Battalion M
    - o   CCCXXXIV Tank Complement Battalion M
- Mixed Depot Italian Islands Troops Aegean (Barletta).

As for self-propelled artillery units, there were 3 Regiments operating in Italy:

- 131st Artillery Regiment for Armored Division (Livorno):
    - o   51st Self-propelled Battery
- 132nd Armored Division Artillery Regiment (Rovereto, in the province of Trento):
    - o   52nd Self-propelled Battery
    - o   54th Self-propelled Battery

---

1 This company should have been equipped with M tanks and sent to the Dodecanese, where the CCCXII Mixed Tank Battalion was operating, in July 1943, but the transfer did not take place due to the evolution of the war events.

- 133$^{rd}$ Armored Division Artillery Regiment (Mantua):
  - o  53$^{rd}$ Self-propelled Battery
  - o  DLV Self-propelled Group

Other units equipped with armored vehicles were also present in the country:
- Training Center of Civitavecchia (it had 15 tanks)
- Central School of Infantry in Rome (had 4 tanks)
- Depot Parachute Troops of Viterbo:
  - o  184$^{th}$ Infantry Platoon (had 6 tanks)
- XXX Tank Battalion
- DCI Self-propelled Group
- DCII Self-propelled Group
- DCIII Self-propelled Group
- DCIV Self-propelled Group
- DCV Self-propelled Group

The large armored units of the Royal Army deployed at home were:
- 135$^{th}$ Armored Division "Ariete II"
- 136$^{th}$ Armored Division "Centauro II"

The only Armored Division available for war use and fully operational in its personnel and its means was the 135$^{th}$ Armored Division "Ariete II", reconstituted after the annihilation of its armored units in Tunisia. This Division, commanded by General Raffaele Cadorna, was dislocated in the surroundings of Rome, but no destination in the war[2] zone was foreseen. In Lazio was also located the 136$^{th}$ Armored Division "Centauro II", which was experiencing a profound phase of reorganization and "political cleansing", after the arrest of Mussolini (July 25, 1943) and the consequent reshuffling of the command cadre of the Milizia Volontaria di Sicurezza Nazionale, of which the former 1$^{st}$ Armored Division "M" was part[3]. As for the Cavalry weapon, the Depots of the following units were located on the Peninsula:

- Nizza Cavalleria (Turin)
- Cavalleggeri di Monferrato(Voghera, province of Pavia)
- Lancieri di Novara (Verona)
- Lancieri di Vittorio Emanuele II (Bologna)
- Lancers of Milan (Civitavecchia, province of Rome)
- Cavalleggeri di Alessandria (Codròipo, province of Udine).

---

2 In reality the Division "Ariete II" should have been sent to Sicily, where the Allies had landed, but just as the first aliquots arrived in Rome in the second half of 1943, Mussolini was deposed and the Division was dislocated around the capital. In the days following the arrest of Mussolini, the Division was put on alert and its units employed in tasks of public order.
3 The 1$^{st}$ Armored Division Black Shirts "M" had been formed in May 1943, as the elite armored division of the fascist regime, equipped with armaments and armored vehicles supplied directly by the Germans. On July 25, the Division was located north of Rome and was still in full training. After having been initially named Divisione Corazzata Legionaria (Legionary Armored Division), the large unit was definitively renamed 136$^{th}$ Armored Division "Centauro II" and placed under the command of General Giorgio Carlo Calvi di Bergolo, son-in-law of King Vittorio Emanuele III, who worked to integrate the Division into the structure of the Royal Army, at the same time purging it of markedly fascist elements. For further information on the history of the Division: "Come il diamante" and "I Tankers di Mussolini - Il gruppo corazzato "Leonessa" dalla M.V.S.N. alla R.S.I." (works cited in bibliography).

Let's take a step back and go back to July 25, 1943, the day of Mussolini's arrest, when General Vittorio Ambrosio, Chief of General Staff, established the "Corpo d'Armata Motocorazzato" (Armored Motorcycle Corps - C.A.M.), formed by three mobile Divisions and an Infantry Division, under the command of General Giacomo Carboni[4]. Officially the Army Corps was organized to defend the Capital in case of an Allied landing, but in reality General Ambrosio wanted to have well-equipped troops to counter any reaction of the fascists, supported by the Germans, after the news of the Duce's capture. The C.A.M. was formed by:

- 21st Infantry Division "Grenadiers of Sardinia", on which these armored units depended:
    - o Motorised Department of Army Corps Command
    - o Depot and Training Battalion
    - o 4th Tanker's Regiment
- 10th Motorized Infantry Division "Piave".[5]
- 135th Armored Division "Ariete II"
- 136th Armored Division "Centauro II"
- Army Corps Troops
    - o 18th Re.C.O. Bersaglieri
    - o 1st Regiment Artillery Celere
    - o 1st Anti-Aircraft Artillery Regiment
    - o 11th Corps Engineer Regiment
    - o 135th Engineer Company
    - o 83rd Engineer Telegraph and Radio Telegraph Company
    - o Army Corps Services

To these units were added, in the tragic moments of the Armistice, units of the 13th Infantry Division "Re" and of the 7th Infantry Division "Lupi di Toscana", which were deployed in an arc around Rome, with maneuver tasks in the northern and southern sectors. The C.A.M. was arranged on a wide elliptical front, which should have allowed to control every access way to Rome and to defend the city itself in case of attack. The "Ariete II" Division was deployed in the north-west, between Manziana, Bracciano and Villa Olgiata, the "Piave" Division in the north-east, between Via Cassia and Via Tiburtina, the "Granatieri di Sardegna" Division and the Re.C.O. of the "Ariete" Division controlled the southern sector, between Via Collatina and Via Boccea, while the "Centauro II" Division was located in the east, between Via Tiburtina and Via Collatina. The latter assumed a secondary position not only because it was undergoing reorganization, but also because it was feared that the soldiers of the unit, largely coming from the M.V.S.N., could deploy in support of the German armed forces in case of a reversal of alliances[6].

The "Ariete II" Division was reconstituted on April 1st in Ferrara, after the almost total destruction of the 132nd Armored Division "Ariete" during the North Africa Campaign, as an

4 Some sources date the establishment of the C.A.M. to 4 days earlier, July 21.
5        The "Piave" had, among other things, a 90/53 Autocannon Group.
6 The "Centauro II", while considered to be unreliable, could have had a strong influence in the defense of Rome, by virtue of the modern German equipment with which it was armed.

Armored Cavalry Division. "Ariete II" had been transferred to the Olgiata area in August, but was still under-organized and included:

- Command
- Command Squadron
- 10° Reggimento Corazzato "Lancieri di Vittorio Emanuele II" (equipped with 5 M40 tanks, 65 M42 tanks, 12 M42 Centro Radio tanks, 71 self-propelled 75/18 M42 tanks, 7 M42 self-propelled command tanks) [7]
- 16° Reggimento Motorizzato "Cavalleggeri di Lucca" (on 1 M42 Self-propelled Squadron and 3 Squadron Groups with 24 self-propelled 75/18 M41 and M42 and 1 command tank)
- 8° Regiment "Lancieri di Montebello" (as scouting unit) [8]
- Depot of the "Lancieri di Firenze" Regiment
- X Complementary Group (on M42 tanks)
- 135th Armored Artillery Regiment (12 self-propelled 75/34 M42)
- 235th Self-propelled Artillery Regiment (equipped with self-propelled 105/25 M43)
- CXXXV Self-propelled Counter-Tank Battalion
- XXXV Mixed Engineer Battalion.

The Division also had a total of 42 armored cars, 252 motorcycles, 48 anti-aircraft guns and 36 artillery pieces. The Armored Division "Centauro II" was none other than the 1st Armored Division "M", made up of personnel of the Milizia Volontaria di Sicurezza Nazionale. Commanded, as we have seen, by General Giorgio Carlo Calvi di Bergolo, it was equipped with 36 German tanks and self-propelled guns, given by the German Armed Forces at the time of the constitution of what was to become the elite division of the Royal Army. The Division was formed by:

- Command
- Command Company
- Carabinieri Company
- Road Movement Unit
- 306th Military Post Office
- Divisional Department
- 131st Carrier Infantry Regiment on:

---

7 The theoretical staff of the Regiment "Lancieri di Vittorio Emanuele II" was to be of 65 M 15/42 tanks and 48 self-propelled 75/18 on three Groups, one of which was intended, starting from September 1, 1943, to provide the recruits, mounted on M15 tanks. On the eve of September 8, the Regiment was stationed near Lake Bracciano and had started towards Rome only 2 self-propelled Squadrons.

8 It had 20 L40 self-propelled vehicles in the II Squadron Group, divided between the Command Squadron and the 6th Squadron. At the R.E.Co. was subsequently detached the DC Group of the 235th Artillery Regiment, under the command of Major Giuliano Lorenzo, with 2 batteries of 105/25 self-propelled vehicles. This was the only unit of the Royal Army to employ the new self-propelled vehicles in operations. The Group had been formed only three months earlier, as the 3rd Group of the 235th Regiment of Artillery Tanks and Self-Propelled Artillery, and was based at Fort Boccea in Rome.

- o   "Leonessa" Tanks Group [9]
- o   XIX Tank Battalion (M15/42) [10]
- Motorized Legionary Regiment (former Battalion Groups "M" "Tagliamento" and "Montebello")
- 136th Artillery Regiment (former Artillery Regiment "Valle Scrivia")
- 136th Mixed Engineer Battalion
- Health Unit
- Core Subsistence
- Commissariat Office

The Division was considered particularly unreliable, due to the strongly political connotation of the majority of its personnel. On September 3rd, the commander himself expressed himself with these words to General Carboni, commander of the Armored Corps: "[...] *in case of emergency, an emergency that can be easily understood after the examination of the situation made by Excellency Carboni, the Centauro can be relied upon relatively. The Centauro is ready to fire against the Anglo-Americans and the Communists, but against the Germans it will never open fire*". For this reason, on the 6th, the Division received the order to defend the Guidonia airport, in order to distance it from the defensive perimeter of Rome.

At the date of the Armistice, elements of the 18th Bersaglieri Regiment, equipped with L6 tanks and AB41 armored cars[11], were also arriving from Turin to be aggregated to the "Centauro II" Division, which was organized on:

- Command
- LXVIII Battalion on:
    - o   Command Company (reinforced by an armored car platoon)
    - o   1st AB41 Armored Car Company (on 4 Platoons for a total of 24 armored cars)
    - o   2nd Tank Company L6/40 (on 4 Platoons for a total of 26 tanks)
    - o   3rd Tank Company L6/40 (on 4 Platoons for a total of 24 tanks)
    - o   4th Motorcycle Company
- LXIX Battalion on:
    - o   Command Company
    - o   5th Company Self-propelled 47/32 L40 (on 2 Platoons for a total of 10 self-propelled)
    - o   6th Truck Company (4 platoons of 20mm anti-aircraft machine guns)

---

9 Organized on:
- 1st Tank Company on 12 Panzer IV Ausf. G
- 2nd Tank Company on 12 Panzer III Ausf. N
- 3rd Self-propelled Company on 12 Sturmgeschütz III Ausf. G

10 The Battalion, although provided for in the staff, never reached the Division, since at the date of the Armistice it was still moving towards Lazio.

11 The Regiment, organized as R.E.Co., consisted of:
- Command and Platoon Command
- LXVIII Bersaglieri Battalion
- LXIX Bersaglieri Battalion.

The Regiment had set out from Turin between the 7th and the 8th of September, traveling on three train convoys. One of these, carrying part of the LXVIII Battalion, found itself blocked at the Florence railway station on September 8. On board were part of the 3rd Company (on L6/40 tanks), the 4th Motorcycle Company and the 5th Self-propelled Company L40. The tanks were unloaded from the railroad cars on the afternoon of September 9 and were driven over the Apennine passes of Futa and Giogo, where they succeeded in slowing down for a few hours the advance of the 24th Panzerdivision, which was aiming at the Tuscan capital from Bologna. The other two rail convoys reached Rome the day of the Armistice: the Regimental Command Company and the Services left the train at the station of Bassano in Teverina, reaching with their own means the area of Settecamini, between Rome and Tivoli[12], where the 1st Platoon of the Armored Car Company AB41, the 2nd Tank Company L6/40 and half of the 3rd Tank Company L6/40 were already located, while the 2nd Platoon AB41 was displaced in Orte[13].

After the announcement of the Armistice, the German armed forces unleashed in the Peninsula the Operation Axis (“*Fall Achse*”), a plan developed by the Oberkommando der Wehrmacht since May, in anticipation of a probable collapse of Fascism. The plan foresaw the neutralization of the Italian armed forces in all the war theaters of the Mediterranean and the military occupation of the Italian territory, resorting to rapid attack operations. The Germans had an easy time of it, in fact the proclamation of Marshal Badoglio was rather equivocal and by many soldiers, even of high rank, was wrongly interpreted as the announcement of the end of the war. This provoked a general disbandment, exacerbated by the lack of precise orders from the High Command, and in all fronts where there were Italian units a collective hysteria was created. Deprived of precise indications, the Italian soldiers were easy prey to the German armed forces, which captured about 815,000 soldiers in the weeks immediately following. More than half of the soldiers on duty in the metropolitan area abandoned their weapons and tried to return home, even disguising themselves in civilian clothes, for fear of German retaliation, which, in fact, did not take long to arrive.

At the same time, however, a small part of the armed forces remained faithful to King Vittorio Emanuele III and tried to oppose the German military reaction, sometimes to the limit of its operational capacity. The reactions of the Tankers and Cavalry units were scarce, most of the units in Italy and in the Balkans were disarmed practically without injury and limited were the episodes of reaction to the German plan of occupation by tank units. On the contrary, there was a decisive counterattack by tank units in Rome, Parma, Piacenza, Piombino, Sardinia and Corsica.

---

12 The “Centauro II” Division was stationed in this area.
13 A Platoon of the Autoblindo Company remained in France at the disposal of the Nice Square Command.

# DISPOSITION OF THE ITALIAN AND GERMAN ARMY FORCES IN THE SURROUNDINGS OF ROME ON SEPTEMBER 8, 1943

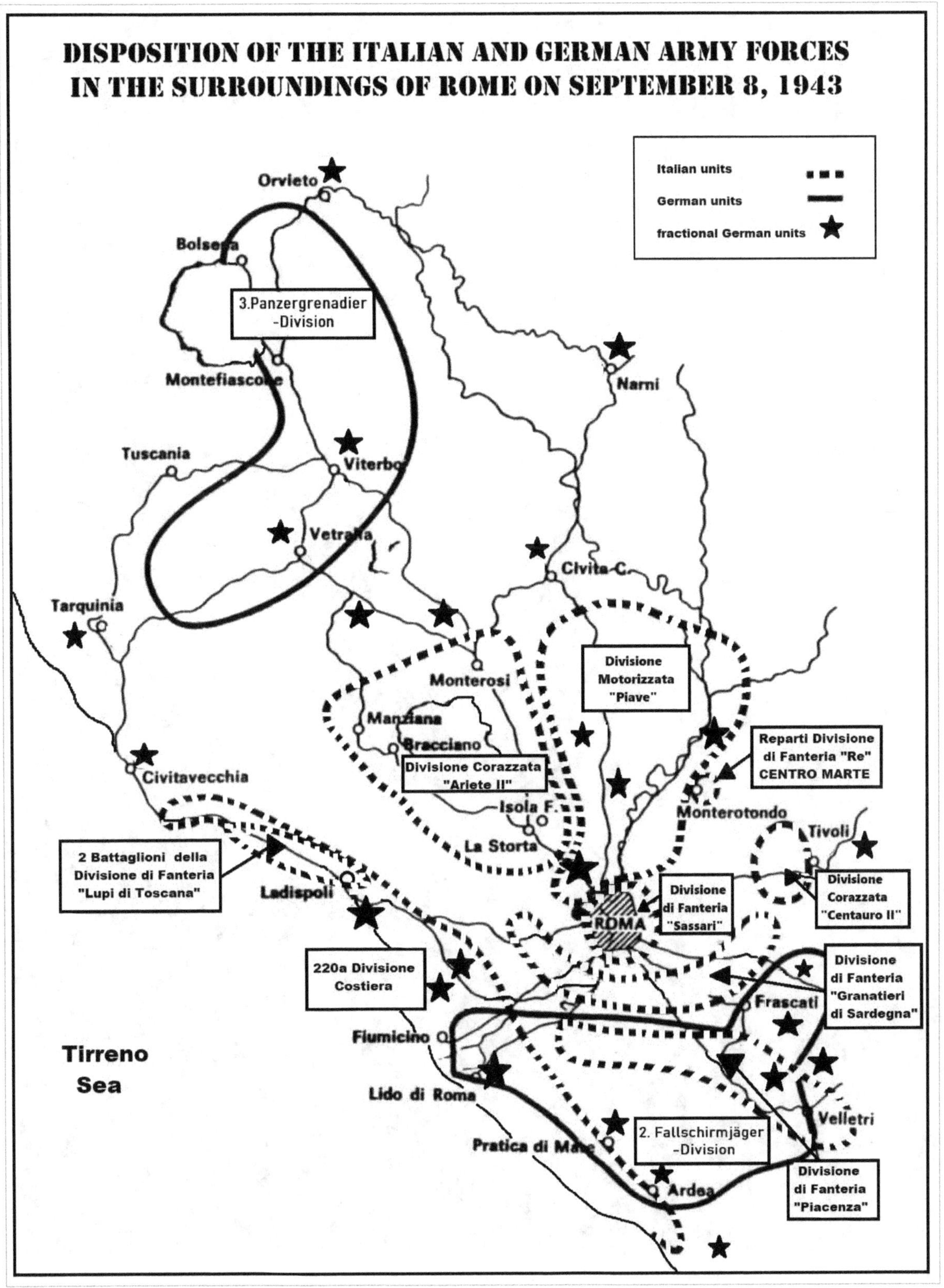

▲ One of the AB41s of the Cheren Column of the Italian Africa Police.

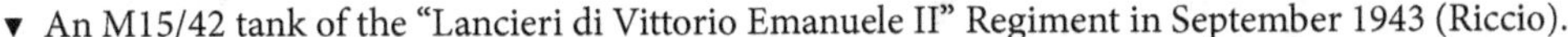

▲ Train convoy stopped near the station of Rome Orte loaded with armored car AB 41 of the Regiment "Lancieri di Montebello", during the transfer from Ferrara to Castelnuovo di Porto (Rome) in July 1943.

▼ An M15/42 tank of the "Lancieri di Vittorio Emanuele II" Regiment in September 1943 (Riccio).

▲ The platoon commanded by Lieutenant Gray de Cristoforis of the 2nd Armored Car Squadron of the "Lancieri di Montebello" stopped at Orte. The lieutenant will distinguish himself during the defense of the capital in the days following the Armistice.

▲ The 4th Carristi Regiment provided some of its tanks, such as this worn-out M13/40, to enable the training of tank hunter units on the outskirts of Rome (Crippa).

▼ The armored car of Lieutenant Fortunato of the "Lancieri di Montebello" in service of public order, after the fall of Fascism (Galeazzi).

▲ Armored car of the Regiment "Lancieri di Montebello" in transfer to Olgiata (Rome) in August 1943, following the killing of Ettore Muti. The political events of July 1943 led to the decision to concentrate the most modern and reliable troops of the Regio near Rome, for the defense of the Capital from any possible internal (the fascists) and external (the Germans) danger (Manes).

▼ Captain Bruno Mei, commander of the Motorcycle Squadron of the "Lancieri di Montebello", photographed next to a FIAT 508 CM car in 1943 (Manes).

▲ Paratroopers and tank drivers of the 4th Regiment during an anti-tank training course near Rome in the summer of 1943 (Crippa).

▲ King Vittorio Emanuele II on board the ship "Baionetta", while repairing towards Brindisi in the night between 8 and 9 September. Together with him General Puntoni and Admiral De Courten (Arena).

▲ Following the announcement of the Armistice, in some cities of the peninsula there were popular demonstrations, sometimes very colorful. In this image, units of the Regio Esercito stationed in Milan, assisted by an L3 tank, intervene in Corso Buenos Aires to keep assemblies of civilians under control (Pisanò).

▼ In the moments following the announcement of the Armistice, confusion reigned supreme among the soldiers in this Bologna barracks, as in the many other military facilities where Italian soldiers were stationed, both at home and abroad.

▲ In the Lombard capital, for fear of a German armed reaction, armed posts were set up to protect the main places of the city: in this case we are near Via Brera (Pisanò).

▲ Many were the divisions that disbanded on September 8th and many were the soldiers who tried to reach their families, convinced that the war was finally over. A group of Bersaglieri set out for Milan's Central Station, fully equipped and armed, in search of a train that could take them home (Pisanò).

▼ The Cheren Column of the Italian Africa Police (Battalion "Vittorio Bottego") on the Mentana - Monterotondo road. The unit was equipped with L6/40 tanks and AB41 armored cars.

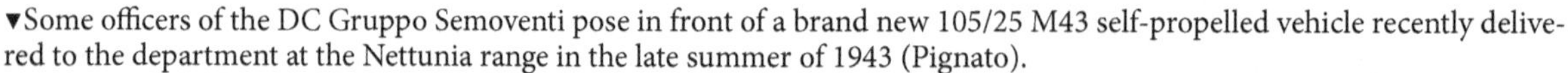

▲ Close-up of the same department of the Italian Africa Police as in the previous photograph: 3 L6 tanks and 1 AB41 can be seen.

▼Some officers of the DC Gruppo Semoventi pose in front of a brand new 105/25 M43 self-propelled vehicle recently delivered to the department at the Nettunia range in the late summer of 1943 (Pignato).

# THE BATTLE FOR ROME

At the time of the Armistice, the Rome Army Corps of General Alberto Barbieri was present in the city of Rome. It consisted, among other things, of the 12th Infantry Division "Sassari", which had the XII Semoventi Battalion from 47/32, under the command of Captain Giuffrè, three motorized battalions of the "Cheren" Column of the Italian African Police and the Motorized Assault Battalion. There were also logistic, training and garrison units, the Depot of the 4th Tankers Regiment, personnel of the Difesa Contraerea Territoriale (Anti-Aircraft Defense - Di.Ca.T), the Air Force, Navy, Royal Guard of Finance and Carabinieri. However, the 4th Tankers had an assortment of vehicles, since the unit had a training function: 31 tanks and 11 self-propelled guns in the Mixed Training Battalion (formerly the 11th Tank Battalion), commanded by Lieutenant Colonel Luigi Battisti, and about twenty trucks[14].

The "Cheren" Column of the P.A.I. had been constituted in the spring of 1943, to be sent to Tunisia, and was a motorized and armored unit of the consistency of an Armored Exploring Unit (R.E.Co.). Given the negative development of the campaign in North Africa, the "Cheren" was deployed in the capital, in anticipation of possible war events that could have occurred in the city. After Mussolini's arrest, it was attached to the Rome Army Corps, functionally aggregated to the Royal Army, and was used for public order tasks in the city. Commanded by Colonel Toscano, it had a staff of about 1,300 men[15] and at the moment of Badoglio's announcement it remained compact, turning its weapons against the Germans.

The Motorized Assault Battalion was derived from the Military Center "A", a unit that brought together Arab and Italian volunteers who were to operate as infiltrators in foreign territory and was part of the "Red Arrows" Regiment. In August 1943 the unit was reorganized into the Motorized Assault Battalion with two Rifle Companies and one Scout Company[16]. The unit was stationed near the Ministry of War with tasks of public order.

---

14 There were only 5 M13/40 tanks, the other tanks were all L3s. Other authors, not citing the sources from which they would have drawn, give a very different indication of the equipment of the 4th Tankers Regiment: 31 M15 tanks and 9 self-propelled 75's, reporting also the presence of an unidentified Gruppo Battaglioni Addestramento Capisquadra with 25 tanks of unidentified type. However, the numerous photographs taken during and after the clashes in Rome clearly show that the 4th Tankers did not have M15/42 tanks.

15 The Cheren Column was organized on:
- Command
- Savoy Battalion
- Bottego" Battalion
- Ruspoli" Battalion
- Blindo Company - Battleship

This Company had 12 L6/40 tanks, 12 AB41 armored cars, 6 47/32 anti-tank guns and 6 Breda 20mm machine guns. Each of the three Battalions consisted of 3 Companies (numbered 7th through 15th).

16 This Company was organized on:
- Command Platoon (with an unspecified number of Model 43 Desert Trucks and 3 AS42 Metropolitan Trucks)
- 1st Truck Platoon (with 6 AS42 Metro trucks)
- 2nd Truck Platoon (with 6 AS42 Metro trucks)
- 3rd Truck Platoon (with 6 AS42 Metro trucks)

After the clashes in Rome, part of the unit's personnel joined the P.A.I., taking with it the surviving trucks. It is probable that the Company also had one or more Desert Trucks Model 43, a development of the Saharan AS37 truck, produced in an unspecified number of units, not to be confused with the AS43 truck.

Around the city was deployed the Armored Army Corps, which had at its disposal numerous armored vehicles and consisted of the aforementioned 135th Armored Division "Ariete II", 10th Motorized Infantry Division "Piave", 136th Motorized Infantry Division "Centauro II" and 21st Infantry Division "Granatieri Sardegna", 136th Armored Division "Centauro II" and 21st Infantry Division "Granatieri di Sardegna", and was reinforced by the 103rd Motorized Infantry Division "Piacenza", by the 220th and 221st Coastal Divisions and finally by the X Regiment Arditi, units that had joined the C. A.M. in the previous week. In addition, for several days along the Via Tiburtina, numerous motor-armored garrisons of the Italian African Police had been deployed in defense of the roadway: in this way, the P.A.I. had full control of the highway from Rome to Avezzano. Even if officially this distribution of garrisons had only a training function, it is very likely that this device was actually taken to keep a possible escape route clear for the King and the Government, a route that was then actually chosen to safely reach Pescara, where the Government embarked on the corvette "Baionetta" towards Brindisi, and Ortona, the place of embarkation of the royal family[17]. Probably also the Armored Division "Ariete II" had been positioned in the area of Tivoli to protect the column that would have transported the Royal Family and the Government.

For the internal defense of the Capital and of the access areas to it there was the 17th Army Corps, under the command of General Giovanni Zanchieri, formed by the 103rd Infantry Division "Piacenza", by the 220th and by the 221st Coastal Division, displaced from the Colli Albani to the sea, with headquarters in Velletri. The Army General Staff of General Mario Roatta, based in Monterotondo, coordinated all these troops, which were not organized in an Army Command.

The total number of Italian forces available for the defense of Rome amounted to 88,137 men, 124 tanks, 257 self-propelled guns, 122 armored cars and Saharan trucks and 615 artillery pieces. It was a complex of heterogeneous forces, but numerous and including well-equipped units (such as the "Ariete II" and "Sassari" Divisions) or solidly framed units (such as the "Granatieri di Sardegna" or the X Arditi Regiment), which, if used in a decisive and unified manner, could have validly countered the German forces present in the area.

The Germans, in fact, had in the area, in addition to the personnel in transit to the south and a small number of police, liaison and support personnel present in the city and at the military installations and communication routes with the front, only two large units, grouped in the XI Airborne Army Corps of General Kurt Student. The first of them was the 2. Fallschirmjäger-Division, commanded by Lieutenant Colonel Wolfgang Meder-Eggebert (who was succeeded a few days later by General Walter Barenthinn) and strong with more than 12,000 men, and was stationed south of Rome, at Pratica di Mare. The Division, which had to defend, in addition to that important airport, the area of Frascati, where Field Marshal Albert Kesselring, Oberbefehlshaber Süd, and Field Marshal Wolfram von Richthofen's Luftflotte 2. were based, had a limited armored component consisting of a company of Marder II tank destroyers, most of which remained in position at Frascati[18]. There was also

---

17 During the navigation from Ortona, the "Baionetta" was then reached by the small modern cruiser "Scipione Africano", which sailed urgently from Taranto.
18 The Division, composed of four regiments (the 2nd, 6th and 7th Paratroopers and the 2nd Parachute Artillery Regiment), to which were added the 2nd Parachute Counter Battalion, the 2nd Battalion of the Parachute Engineer Corps, various

the 3. Panzergrenadier-Division of General Fritz-Hubert Gräser, located north of Rome in the area between Orvieto and Lake Bolsena, which had 3 Panzer III command tanks, 42 StuG III 75mm assault guns, 18 Wespe self-propelled guns, several dozen wheeled and half-tracked armored vehicles, with a staff of about 10,000 men. Finally, at the disposal of the Division there was also the Kampfgruppe "Büssing", formed by the command of Panzer-Regiment 26 and its Companies 5, 6 and 7, by the III.Abteilung of Panzer-Artillerie-Regiment 93 and by the II.Bataillon of Panzergrenadier-Regiment 67. The Kampfgruppe lined up 2,200 men, about 30 Panzer IIIs, about 60 Panzer IVs, 24 artillery pieces and 20 20mm machine guns. There was, finally, the 15. Panzergrenadier-Division of general Eberhard Rodt, which had few armored vehicles, destined to protect the area between Gaeta and the Volturno river, ready to rush quickly to the area of Salerno, where the 16. Panzer-Division was dislocated, with only one armored battalion, where an Allied landing[19] was feared. Finally, there were German divisions at the Castelli Romani for the defense of the German headquarters, and Flak personnel assigned to the numerous anti-aircraft batteries of the Luftwaffe, integrated in the Italian anti-aircraft defense.

In the area of Rome, therefore, the situation of the opposing forces saw on the evening of the 8th a clear Italian supremacy in men and means of all kinds. The absolute lack of a homogeneous plan of attack and of timely orders from the Government and from the Armed Forces' General Staff, whose leaders took the path of personal salvation in the South, and the overestimation of the enemy forces by our intelligence services, meant that the actions of the Royal Army units, unfortunately, were fragmentary and ineffective everywhere.

The Armistice proclamation did not foresee any offensive attack against the Germanic forces present on the national territory and around Rome, but since the end of August, the Chief of Staff General Ambrosio had elaborated for the Armed Forces the secret directive "O.P. Memoria 44", which ordered "to interrupt at any cost, also with attacks in force to the armed protection units, the railways and the main Alpine railways" and to "act with large units or mobile groupings against the German troops". At first, however, both General Ambrosio and General Roatta were convinced that the German army would have given up occupying the Capital, retreating instead without fighting towards the north and therefore the commander of the Armored Corps did not alert his units.

On the contrary, the military reaction of the German Wehrmacht forces was rapid, according to the operative directives established by Adolf Hitler in case of Italian defection ("Operation Achse"), so much so that around 11:00 p.m. more and more reports of aggressive actions of the German troops began to reach the Army General Staff, both in the Rome area and in many other parts of Italy and abroad; the requests for precise instructions on how to behave towards the former ally were also more and more frantic. General Ambrosio, however, decided not to activate immediately the famous secret directive "O.P. Memoria 44". At that moment, however, Rome was already under siege: the German 2. Fallschirmjäger-Divi-

---

services and the Armed Company with 11 self-propelled Marder II fighters and 42 anti-tank guns), had been transferred from the OKW to Rome by air between 26 and 28 July 1943, in anticipation of rebellion movements following the fall of Mussolini.

19 The armored vehicles of the two large German units (about 180) were therefore numerically inferior to the Italian ones, but SIM, on the other hand, had provided erroneous information, which made the number of German tanks present near Rome rise to about 600.

sion had moved towards the city from Pratica di Mare airport and the fighting had already begun at 22:00 near the Magliana bridge, the 3.Panzergrenadier-Division started to advance towards Viterbo from Montefiascone, while the troops displaced in the Castelli Romani moved towards Velletri, where the Command of the 17th Italian Army Corps was located.

In fact, General Albert Kesselring had initially expected a landing in Lazio, but since this did not occur, around 10:00 p.m. he had given orders to Student and Greaser to overthrow the Italian defenses established along the coast from Formia to Civitavecchia and in short order the 220th Coastal Division was disarmed. After having essentially put out of action also the Infantry Division "Piacenza" and the remaining Coastal forces, Kesselring began to press toward Rome, with the 3rd Armored Grenadier Division from the north and the 2nd Parachute Division from the south, employing also units of the 15th Infantry Division, which had been assigned to Salerno, whose elements occupied Fondi on the Appian Way.

▲ Exercise of self-propelled 75/18, probably of the "Ariete II" Division in the Roman countryside, between Guidonia and Bagni di Tivoli, in the days before the Armistice (Arena).

▲ A division of 75/18 self-propelled vehicles approaches Rome in anticipation of a possible German military reaction.

▼ AB41 armored car and motorcyclists of the "Montebello" in the Roman countryside (Manes).

▲ AB41 of the "Lancieri di Montebello" Regiment overtaken by a group of motorcyclists (Manes).

▲ Another image of the column of AB41 of the "Lancieri di Montebello" moving towards Rome (Manes).

▼AB41 armored car of the "Lancieri di Montebello" Regiment on the eve of the clashes in the Capital.

▲ A group of people are curiously observing an AB41 armored car, which is taking position on the streets of the capital. The climate is still quiet, civilian cars are circulating and a city vigilante, in the typical uniform with the characteristic white helmet, directs the traffic, as in a normal day.

▲ In an atmosphere still of apparent tranquility, a 75/18 self-propelled truck quickly crosses Via del Corso, in the middle of the city center.

▲ On the morning of September 9, 1943, in a street in the center of Rome, probably Corso Vittorio Emanuele, a self-propelled car, a FIAT 508 and a CL39 lorry pass quickly, observed by a group of inhabitants of the capital. Despite the fact that there is a military post in front of the building in the foreground, the atmosphere still seems relaxed, even public transport is circulating regularly.

▼ An AB41 of the "lancieri di Montebello" guards an intersection in the capital on the morning of September 9. Some curious passers-by look out the open doors of the vehicle to see inside; the armored car has the license plate "RE 545 B".

▲ A 47/32 self-propelled vehicle, probably belonging to the 4th Carristi Regiment, followed by an OM Taurus truck loaded with soldiers, moving through the streets of Rome. The situation is so surreal that a Wehrmacht car is quietly parked by the side of the road.

▲ The 10th Company of the 1st Regiment "Granatieri di Sardegna" while taking position in the Magliana area on September 9, 1943.

▼ Lieutenant Spalletti and Sergeant Zanenga of the "Montebello" Regiment attempted a courageous lightening raid at Montagnola, but their armored cars were hit by the precise counter-tank fire of the German paratroopers. As you can clearly see from this picture, one of the two armored cars was under the fire of three PaK36 anti-tank guns of the German paratroopers.

# SEPTEMBER 9, 1943

After 4:00 a.m. of September 9, with the battle in progress and unbeknownst to his superior Vittorio Ambrosio, General Mario Roatta, Chief of Staff of the Royal Army, ordered to General Giacomo Carboni, commander of the Armored Corps, to move to Tivoli the 135th Armored Division "Ariete II" and the 10th Infantry Division "Piave"[20]. The commanders of the two Divisions, who were already in contact with the German avant-garde, were stunned by this order, which appeared to be a retreat, so much so that they initially refused to follow the directives. In reality this order is clear if considered together with what happened only an hour later. In fact, shortly after 5:00 a.m., King Vittorio Emanuele III and his family, Prime Minister Marshal Badoglio, Chiefs of Staff Ambrosio and Roatta, and the Military Ministers took the road to Brindisi, leaving the country in disarray, passing along a route that, in fact, remained protected by the two Divisions that had just been moved. The situation in Rome was precipitating. In fact, the Italian units disposed on the coast had already been neutralized by the German blows and the order of retreat toward Tivoli of all the Divisions of the device of protection of the Capital, excluding only the "Granatieri di Sardegna", that was already under attack, represented in fact a renunciation to the defense of the city[21].

At 5:15 a.m. Army Chief of Staff De Stefanis issued this order to the Armoured Corps and, for information, to the Army Corps Command in Rome:

*"Taking orders from Supreme Command, I communicate:*

*I - East situation such as to exclude a long resistance of the troops stationed around the capital against the Germanic troops marching on it. On the other hand, a prolonged resistance would expose city and citizenry to serious and severe losses.*

*II - Consequently, the troops currently employed in the defense of Rome (external and internal) that you take all at your orders fall back on Tivoli and the adjacent region.*

*Ili - Fall back in staggered fashion, in order, having the set preceded by units taking up position facing east[22], straddling Tivoli.*

*IV - Orient yourself to continue then possibly eastward.*

---

20 There has been much debate on the reasons behind this order, which in fact made the defensive complex around the capital more vulnerable. According to some, the decision was taken to create a cordon of containment to a possible advance from the south of the German Armed Forces, according to others the position taken by the two Divisions would have served to cover the escape of the royal family to Abruzzo, in case of German attacks. In fact, the royal convoy, composed of seven cars, could "miraculously" reach its destination, after having traveled 200 km without being bothered by any German military unit. Some historians even claim that, while the concentration order was being issued towards Tivoli, the Chief of General Staff negotiated with General Kesselring the evacuation of the authorities in exchange for the neutralization of the Italian armed forces. It is also plausible that this movement aimed to avoid transforming the Capital into a battlefield, which would have caused the destruction of monuments and religious institutions dependent on the Vatican.
21 In the hours immediately following the announcement of the Armistice, to the south of the Capital, German paratroopers had seized the fuel depots of Mezzocamino and Vallerano, where 16,000 liters of gasoline were at the disposal of the Army General Staff, by simply showing up with the excuse of refueling, quickly putting the small guard division of the "Piacenza" Division out of action. Almost at the same time the 222nd Coastal Division, deployed between Nettunia and Fregene, was routed by German soldiers who had entered the camps by surprise. In the first hours of September 9, also the Division "Piacenza", despite the resistance of several strongholds was forced to retreat.
22 This is an obvious error, as the correct direction was west.

*V - In the city of Rome, the units of the CC.RR. and the Police must remain, for the maintenance of order.*

*VI - Bring your command in full time to Tivoli, where you will make contact with us.*

*The Chief of Staff of the Army."*

This order, however, was not considered valid and the C.A.M. decided independently to refer to that one.

previous plan to concentrate at Tivoli in case of offensive operations.

At 7:45 about 800 German paratroopers jumped on the outskirts of Monterotondo, where the so-called "Centro Marte", the country headquarters of the Italian Headquarters at Palazzo Orsini, was located, with the objective of capturing the Army General Staff, which, however, as we have seen had already moved away and, therefore, the paratroopers began to converge on the capital on the morning of the following day, September 10, after having been confronted by units of the "Piave" Division and a Company of the Italian Africa Police, equipped with armored cars, AS42 trucks, L6/40 tanks and flamethrowers.

Between Via Cassia and Via Casilina, the Armored Division "Ariete II" had set up defensive strongholds along a line of 28 km, which were hit several times by German attacks throughout the day of the 9th, attacks regularly repelled with bloody clashes. As a result of this situation, however, almost no unit of the Division could reach the city to participate in the fighting. Around 10:00 a.m. at the Cecchignola armored units of the P.A.I. and of the 4th Tankers Regiment repelled attacks led by German units that were trying to break through.

In the area of Bracciano, Monterosi and Manziana, the Regiment "Cavalleggeri di Lucca", the 6th Squadron Self-propelled guns of the II Group and the 8th Squadron Self-propelled guns of the III Group of the "Lancieri di Vittorio Emanuele II" of the Division "Ariete II" blocked the 3.Panzergrenadier-Division. The Italian units did not retreat, inflicting heavy losses on the Germans, who had asked to pass to reach Rome, and who, denied permission, had attacked with infantry and tanks. The 3.Panzergrenadier-Division was thus forced to bypass the defensive perimeter of the capital from the western side, heading undisturbed south towards the area of Salerno[23]. During the clashes, around noon, a Platoon of the 8th 75/18 Squadron engaged the fight with a German column coming from Manziana and stopped at the "Doganella". The Platoon, firing all available shots, blocked two Panzer IV, hitting the tracks. At that point the self-propelled gun of the Platoon's vice-commander, Sergeant Major Udino Bombieri, was also hit and immobilized. Bombieri, despite being wounded, tenaciously resisted on board of his self-propelled gun, after having moved away his crew, succeeding in making an enemy tank unusable. In order not to expose him to enemy fire, he prevented his Platoon commander from approaching to rescue him and got off the armored vehicle to try to dismantle the machine gun on board. The sergeant-major was then caught from behind by a German soldier, who had gone around the theater of combat,

---

23 The Regiment "Lancieri di Vittorio Emanuele II" lost 10 self-propelled vehicles during the fighting, while the Regiment "Cavalleggeri di Lucca" lost 4 tanks and 20 men.

who shot him dead. Udino Bombieri was awarded the Gold Medal for Military Valor with the following motivation: "*Tank foreman and deputy platoon commander, when he received the order to abandon his self-propelled gun, already wounded, by a Germanic shell, he ordered to the radio operator and the pilot to leave the self-propelled gun and he remained under the enemy barrage to make it completely useless. Hit again by shrapnel, he did not leave the tank until he was sure to leave it completely out of use in the hands of the enemy. Mortally wounded, he signaled to his platoon commander, who was trying to get close to him and bring him help, not to care about him, not to expose himself, to return to his platoon in combat. He kept on firing with his machine gun, until he was caught from behind and killed with revolver shots by German grenadiers - Bracciano, September 9, 1943*". The resistance of the Lancieri continued even after the death of Bombieri by a handful of men, guarding a machine-gun nest near the state road of Bracciano, who continued to resist even after the death of the officer, firing until the shots were exhausted and finally trying to save themselves. Corporal Antonio Merlo tried to return to the position to recover the machine gun, but he was mowed down by the fire of a German MG[24]; two other soldiers were killed nearby, Elia Candido and Enrico Latini. The 8th Squadron of the "Lancieri di Vittorio Emanuele II" fought against the enemy, palm to palm, suffering heavy losses, but allowing the self-transported soldiers of the Regiment "Cavalleggeri di Lucca" to disengage and fall back.

In the meantime the paratroopers of the 2nd German Division, leaving the "Piacenza" Division on their right, advancing on the roads that from the coast converged on Rome, reached the defensive perimeter arranged by the "Granatieri di Sardegna" Division, commanded by the energetic General Gioacchino Solinas. The Division was reinforced, in the EUR area, by the "Lancieri di Montebello" Regiment, which arrived during the night to help with its self-propelled guns[25]. At 23:30 of the previous day, in fact, the Regiment "Montebello" had received notice to move from Olgiata to the city under the dependence of the Division "Granatieri"; the "Montebello" started to march around 02:30, leaving on the spot the III Gruppo Squadroni, guarding the stronghold of Isola Farnese. Through Madonna di Bracciano, La Storta, La Giustiniana, Ponte Milvio and after having bypassed the Colosseum, the "Montebello" reached the defensive line of the "Granatieri", staying close to the line of strongholds garrisoned by the 1st Battalion, between the Tiber and via Ardeatina. Already at 04.00 a.m. on September 9, the Montebello Regiment was in position, in a focal zone, where important arteries converged, leading directly into the city (via del Mare, via Ostiense, via Laurentina, via Ardeatina) and where it was therefore important to preserve the integrity of the defensive line, to avoid a rapid German penetration into the Capital. The III Battalion of the 1st Regiment "Granatieri" was deployed on a system of strongholds called "Numero 5" (placed at the barricade of the Magliana bridge, via del Mare and via Ostiense), "Numero 6" (via Laurentina) and "Numero 7" (at the barricade of via Ardeatina). The "Numero 5" stronghold, held by the 9th Grenadier Company, was lost after a strong attack by the Kampfgruppe von der Heydte, composed by the 1st and 3rd Battalion of the 6th Parachute Regiment and by three Batteries of the 2nd Artillery Regiment, armed with Pak40 of the

---

24 In memory of the graduate, will be awarded the Bronze Medal for Military Valor.
25 These were the 11 L40 self-propelled vehicles of the 6th Squadron. The Division "Ariete II" had in fact retreated towards Tivoli, to retake the stronghold at the Magliana bridge.

2.Fallschirmjäger-Divison, and at 07:00 the "Montebello" received the order to recapture this stronghold, with the support of the 2nd Battalion Allievi Carabinieri. The fights went on non-stop until 10:00, when the position was finally reoccupied. Subsequently, the "Numero 7" position was surrounded by German forces, but the intervention of the Lancieri allowed the attack to be repulsed.  During the night the DC Gruppo Self-propelled guns, commanded by Major Giuliano, had been recalled with the order to reach Garbatella, where an officer of the Granatieri would have given the necessary indications. The Group moved with difficulty[26], but finally Major Giuliano succeeded in communicating with the command of the "Granatieri" Division, which ordered to place a Battery at the "Numero 5" stronghold and all the rest of the Group at the "Numero 6" stronghold. At the "Numero 5" was assigned the 2nd Battery, commanded by Captain Nunzio Incannamorte. During all the day of September 9, the Group at the "Numero 6" stronghold was engaged in finding supplies, while the 2nd Battery was hard engaged in the fights, so much that Major Giuliano, in the attempt to reach it, was seriously wounded.

In the afternoon the P.A.I. withdrew all the units located along Via Tiburtina, channelling them towards Lauretano, where, around 17:00, a new German counterattack began. In the meantime, the strongholds 5 and 7 were again under attack and the "Montebello" launched itself once more against the German forces. On Via Laurentina, at Magliana, the German advance was thwarted by the Lancers of the "Montebello", the combat moved towards the Basilica of San Paolo, while the paratroopers raked the last defenders among the ruins and wreckage. The Germans, in order to gain time, started negotiations with the Italian command and, the absolute lack of reinforcements, the critical situation of fuel and ammunition, pushed the commanders of the "Grenadier Division" to the decision to withdraw the defensive line of 1 km. In the evening, therefore, the "Granatieri" began the orderly retreat towards more internal positions (Forte Ostiense - Via Laurentina - Casa del Fascio - Via Trisulti), in order to give free transit to the German troops on the Magliana bridge, thus allowing them to reach the Via Aurelia to head North without crossing Rome.

The fighting resumed around the hill of EUR district, in Tre Fontane area and at Forte Ostiense; due to contradictory orders coming from the high commands, the Italian troops were not able to arrange an organic defense, but the sacrifice of the "Montebello" allowed to contain the enemy impetus. A Light Tank Formation Company of the 4th Tankers Regiment, clashed with German paratroopers, losing several tanks, some of which were captured and immediately redeployed by German troops.

---

26 The Group, which had contingent problems of fuel, ammunition, and incomplete training, "was still an efficient unit, but one that had reached the limits of its possibilities."

▲ The two AB41 of the Lancieri di "Montebello" destroyed during the battle of Montagnola. The vehicles caught fire and the crews perished in that desperate action.

▼ In the foreground some abandoned Italian motorcycles and, behind them, an AB41 surrounded by German soldiers. The picture was taken at the end of the "Battle of Montagnola", in Via Lurentina near the Coppi Tannery, while soldiers and officers of the German 2. Fallschirmjäger-Division inspected the battlefield, proceeding to the rounding up of soldiers and civilians.

▲ Sergeant Major Udino Bombieri of the 8th Semoventi Squadron of the III Group of the "Lancieri di Vittorio Emanuele II", who fell at Bracciano on September 9.

▲ Sergeant Major Bombieri's self-propelled gun destroyed at the end of the fight. Bombieri's memory was awarded the Gold Medal for Military Valor.

▼ A self-propelled 75/18 of the Regiment "Lancieri di Montebello" destroyed on the Via del Mare during the fighting for the recapture of the stronghold "Numero 5".

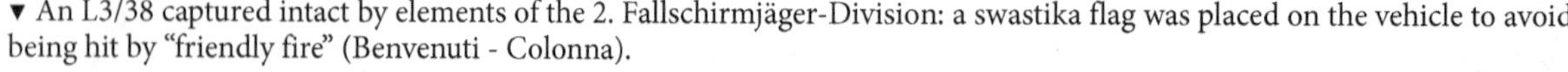

▲ L3 tanks, probably from the 4th Carristi Regiment, abandoned intact at the end of the fighting on September 9, 1943 (Benvenuti - Colonna).

▼ An L3/38 captured intact by elements of the 2. Fallschirmjäger-Division: a swastika flag was placed on the vehicle to avoid being hit by "friendly fire" (Benvenuti - Colonna).

▲ German paratroopers aboard Italian tanks, taken during clashes in the capital.

▼ Conversation between officers of the "Lancieri di Montebello" just arrived at Porta San Paolo. Recognizable are Captain Roselli Lorenzini, Colonel Giordani and, from behind, Captain Mei (Arena).

▲ An AS42 "Metropolitana" truck armed with a 47/32 anti-tank gun of the Motorized Assault Battalion, waiting for the events at Porta San Paolo (Arena).

▼ Among these officers of the "Montebello" we see on the right, in civilian clothes, Raffaele Persichetti. The young man, former lieutenant of the Grenadiers, put on leave because invalid of war, had rushed to Porta San Paolo to resume his place next to his fellow soldiers also in civilian clothes. Summarily armed, he immediately put himself in command of a squad that was left without a guide. Around 14:00, already seriously wounded in the shoulder, he was forced to retreat to the beginning of Viale Giotto, where he died shortly afterwards. The father found the body of his son only after two days of vain searches in the mortuary of the Ospedale del Littorio. His memory was awarded the Gold Medal for Military Valor (Arena).

▲ A 47/32 self-propelled of the 6th Squadron of the Regiment "Lancieri di Montebello" goes to lurk in the arch of Porta San Paolo.

▼ The crew of the self-propelled vehicle apprehensively scrutinizes the situation beyond Porta San Paolo; on the left, an intrigued little girl unconsciously observes what is happening beyond the walls (Pisanò).

▲ From viale Giotto, two 75/18 M42 self-propelled howitzers head towards piazzale Ostiense, where some 100/17 howitzers are already located.

▼ A 75/18 self-propelled vehicle of the 5th Squadron of the "Lancieri di Montebello" near Porta San Paolo; behind it an armored car and some motorcyclists.

# SEPTEMBER 10, 1943

The night between the 9th and the 10th of September passed quietly in the positions of the "Granatieri", barricaded in the Ostiense Fort, and of the "Montebello" Regiment. Around 05:30 a.m. came the news of a truce of arms, agreed by Lieutenant Colonel Giaccone with the Germans, from 07:00 a.m. to 10:00 a.m. Contrary to the agreements made, however, the new positions of the Grenadiers were soon attacked by the German paratroopers, who began to advance towards the center of Rome, carrying out coups, taking advantage of this situation of apparent tranquility. At 06:45 a.m. the Fallschirmjäger attacked the "Numero 8" (Number 8) stronghold, located at km 8 of Via Ardeatina, also supported by armored vehicles, probably Marder self-propelled guns. After an hour of fighting, the situation had become critical for the Italian units and at 08:00 the "Numero 8" stronghold had to fall back on a checkpoint behind, also on the Via Ardeatina, followed after an hour by the "Numero 9" stronghold on the Via Appia. Shortly before 07:00 the Germans attacked from behind the command post of the 1st Regiment "Granatieri", located at the former headquarters of the Fascio Laurentino in Via Trisulti, at Montagnola ("Number 5" stronghold), just as Colonel Mario Di Pierro was reporting to his battalion commanders. This was one of the most famous and raw episodes of the Roman resistance of those days, known as the "Battle of the Montagnola". While the Grenadiers, about 800 men barricaded in the Ostiense Fort, were invested by the German attack, the two AB41 armored cars of Lieutenant Stellato Spalletti and Sergeant Zanenga, of the 1st Squadron of the Regiment "Lancieri di Montebello", carried out a brave lightening raid, but they were hit by the precise anti-tank fire of the German paratroopers and caught fire, causing the death of the crews.

The wounded Italians were received in the houses of Montagnola and treated as best they could by the Franciscan nuns of the Gaetano Giardino Institute, while the battle continued unabated. After the Germans occupied the Ostiense Fort, the fighting continued in the surrounding area of the Montagnola: Grenadiers, Lancers of the "Montebello", a Company of Paratroopers, were supported by many civilians of the area, who had been armed. The center of the Italian resistance was the so-called "red house" (Casa del Fascio Laurentino) and the house of Quirino Roscioni, the baker of the area, already maimed in the Great War, who had taken up arms together with his workers, turning his house and his bakery into the last trench of resistance[27]. Don Pietro Occelli, parish priest of the Montagnola Church, was at the Gaetano Giardino Institute, where about four hundred children, including war orphans and the mentally handicapped, were housed. The Institute was stormed by a group of "green devils", supported by some flamethrowers: Don Pietro had to come out waving a white sheet, explaining to the officer who commanded the German paratroopers that he was in an orphanage and that the soldiers present would cease fire and lay down their weapons. At 08:00 the situation became untenable, given the impossibility of stopping the Germanic infiltration, and the order came for the surviving troops to fall back on the axis

---

27 When the ammunition ran out, Roscioni did his best to save the soldiers, providing them with civilian clothes and waiting for the Germans to arrive with his sister-in-law, D'Angelo Pasqua. The German soldiers chased him out of the house, allowing him to reach the Parish of Montagnola. When they were just a few steps away from the church, they were reached by a machine gun fire, which mortally wounded them. Similarly, seven other parishioners were killed at the doors of the church.

San Paolo - Garbatella - Testaccio, since it was not possible to receive reinforcements, while the "Montebello" had to concentrate in the barracks of Santa Croce in Gerusalemme, leaving a rearguard veil.

In total, at Montagnola, at Fort Ostiense and in the vicinity there were 53 casualties, of which 42 military[28] and 11 civilians.

The surviving armored vehicles of the "Lancieri di Montebello" attempted offensive actions, which were however all crushed, causing the first infiltrations deep into the city of German soldiers. At the same time, in the early morning of September 10, a Company of L tanks, most likely of the 4th Tankers Regiment, was placed in Piazza Venezia, effectively opposing the German attacks for several hours, holding the position.

The "Granatieri" Division was thus concentrated at the Aurelian Walls, near Porta San Paolo, Porta San Sebastiano and Porta San Giovanni, waiting for other units of the C.A.M. to come to help. In the meantime, General Carboni had asked for the intervention of some units of the "Ariete II" Division to support the "Granatieri di Sardegna" Regiment in the area of Porta San Paolo and Ardeatina against the attacks of the 2. Fallschirmjäger-Division, but, considering that the German pressure had increased after having forced the Granatieri and the "Montebello" to retreat from Montagnola, around 10:30 a.m. General Carboni himself ordered the counterattack to the "Granatieri". 1 Infantry Battalion and 1 Group of 100/17 howitzers of the "Sassari" Division came to support the extreme resistance. elements of the V Guastatori, an aliquot of the CCI Battaglione Mortai, armored units of the "Lancieri di Montebello" equipped with armored cars and self-propelled 75/18 M42[29], 2 tank companies of the XI Battaglione of the 4° Reggimento Tanker Infantry, a self-propelled L40 Squadron of the 4th Infantry Fighters Regiment, the 4th Regiment "Genova Cavalleria", elements of the 111th, 122nd and 123rd Companies of the Arditi Camionettisti of the 10th Regiment, as well as Bersaglieri, Carabinieri Cadets of the 2nd Battalion, P. A.I. soldiers and numerous civilian volunteers.A.I. militiamen and numerous civilian volunteers; also some brand new 105/25 M43 self-propelled guns of the DC Gruppo Self-propelled guns, commanded by Major Giuliano Lorenzo, arrived as reinforcement. About 2,000 men of all arms were on site. In spite of the overwhelming superiority of the German troops, the resistance front along the walls of Porta San Paolo raised barricades and even shielded itself with some overturned

---

28  Among them, the fallen of the armored departments were:
- Aldo Bufano
- Camillo Silvio
- Camisani Giacomo
- Chieccher Pio, decorated with Silver Medal for Military Valor to the memory
- Cogliati Rodolfo
- Franchini Francesco
- Solla Alfredo, of the 6° Squadron of the "Lancieri di Montebello", Silver Medal for Military Valor in Memory
- Tincani Vittorio
- Zamboni Edgardo, of the 3rd Motorcycle Squadron of the "Lancieri di Montebello".

They were also found the bodies of 8 tank drivers, unrecognizable because they were charred, and 3 unknown tank drivers fell in front of n. 54 of Via Laurentina. Among the fallen of the Montagnola there was also Captain Nunzio Incannamorte, who, as we will see later, after having positioned himself with his 105/25 self-propelled vehicle to guard the radio transmitting station of the EIAR, was mortally hit near the Ostiense fort.

29 Previously, the unit had been withdrawn first at the barracks of the 13th Artillery Regiment, then in Piazza Santa Croce, because it was believed, erroneously, that the Grenadier Division had reached a "cease-fire" agreement with the adversaries.

streetcar cars on the roadway, while the few vehicles of the "Montebello" found themselves acting in the open. While the armored vehicles of the "Genova Cavalleria" were lining up in Viale Giotto, the old 100/17 guns of the "Sassari" were also positioned in front of Porta San Paolo, whose servants fought tirelessly, supported by the voluntary help of some civilians. The 1st Battery of the DC Gruppo Self-propelled guns, commanded by Captain Vito Santoro, was literally mowed down, so much so that it lost all its officers and all its vehicles, mowed down by the German Pak40 anti-tank guns, during the battle at Porta San Paolo: the Group had previously received the order to deploy along Via dell'Impero, to oppose the Germans coming down Via Cavour, but its intervention was also requested by the Grenadiers. Three self-propelled guns remained in Via dell'Impero, while the other three reached Porta San Paolo. The 2nd Battery of the Group, on the other hand, went to the suburbs in Prato Smeraldo, where its commander Captain Nunzio Incannamorte died. In command of his own 105/25 self-propelled gun, Incannamorte was protecting the radio transmitting station of the EIAR, where he resisted for a long time to the attack of the German troops. His battery tried to break the German encirclement by charging with the remaining vehicles and Captain Incannamorte, on the Via Laurentina, near the Ostiense fort, after running out of ammunition from his tank, managed to overwhelm an enemy position, firing only with the machine gun on board, but was wounded on the Via Laurentina, near the Ostiense fort, and died after being transported to the Celio military hospital. His memory was awarded the Gold Medal for Military Valor[30]. In the meantime, at Porta San Paolo, a division of dismounted recruits from the Rome Depot of the "Genova Cavalleria", commanded by Captain Francesco Vannetti Donnini, fought relentlessly, even though they were soldiers at the beginning of their career, assisted by a large group of civilians. Captain Vannetti Donnini, while he was inciting his boys, was seriously wounded by a grenade, but he continued to fight until the last cartridge, even unholstering his own pistol to face the Germans who were advancing against him, being mowed down by a shot fired at point-blank range to his chest. To the memory of this brave captain was recognized the Gold Medal for Military Valor[31]. During the clashes, Captain Romolo Fugazza of the 8th Regiment "Lancieri di Montebello", commander of a 75/18 self-propelled squadron, was killed in his self-propelled unit and

---

30 This is the motivation: *"Officer of elective military virtues, ardent of patriotism, he had already distinguished himself for exceptional value and for marked ability during long and risky operational cycles in other chessboards. Commander of a self-propelled battery of 105/25, with audacious actions of maneuver and fire, contributed to reject, for a whole day, repeated attacks by German paratroopers, who were uselessly raging against the position firmly held by him. Surrounded and invested by an intense artillery and mortar fire, he did not give up the fight. The next day, in the compelling need to break through the encirclement, he reserved for himself the arduous task of eliminating an anti-tank piece that was blocking the road: with his whole torso out of the wagon and his pistol in his fist, he ventured against the enemy's trap, shattering it in his overwhelming momentum. And while the success crowned his audacity, a machine gun burst hit him in the forehead. Before breathing his last breath, he still found the strength to incite his artillerymen to continue the desperate fight. Consciously, he met a glorious death in an act of supreme dedication to the Homeland. - Rome, September 10, 1943"*.

31 *"Officer of indomitable bravery, he fought in France, Croatia and Russia, where he was already the hero of epic episodes. Fretful for the delineated misfortunes of Italy, he welcomed with joy the repeatedly solicited order to lead his "Genova" dragoons to the baptism of fire in defense of the Capital of Italy. Tireless, he was always in the most delicate and exposed part of his line-up, among his dismounted platoons, bleeding for the continuous losses, animating and attacking the enemy with bombs and machine guns wherever he approached. Careless of himself and caring of his own, he didn't hesitate to replace one of his wounded subordinates in the moment and in the point in which the enemy fire was stronger and more decisive. Severely wounded by a grenade, he imperiously disengaged those who had rushed to support him to send them to get ammunition, and dragged himself to a machine gun to fire the last cartridge. He then stood with his pistol in his fist to face the fast advancing enemy. Hit by a shot fired at point-blank range to his chest, he fell to the ground, nobly sacrificing his life. - Porta San Paolo 10 September 1943"*.

was awarded the Memorial[32] Gold Medal. Lieutenant Silvio Gridelli, from the 4th Tankers Regiment, took part in the Porta San Paolo clashes with a Tank Company M: sent on reconnaissance at the head of a Platoon, he was wounded in the leg, but continued to fight until death and, for this reason, his memory was awarded the Silver Medal for Military Valor[33]. The standard bearer of the Regiment, second lieutenant Raffaello Parri, committed himself for the whole duration of the clashes to the recovery of the wounded. In command of a platoon of L3 light tanks, he worked tirelessly in the rescue operation in the area most affected by German anti-tank fire, thanks to the precious help of Lieutenant Giacomo Rufini and the pilot Corporal Tommaso Pasetti.

Around 3 p.m. the Ostiense square was subjected to a massive concentration of artillery and mortar fire, while the Italian troops concentrated on the left were hit by a heavy machine-gun fire, which created very serious losses. At 4 p.m. the German paratroopers of the 6th Regiment, having passed the Porta Ardeatina, less than one kilometer east of Porta San Paolo, easily reached the Archaeological Promenade and the area behind the Baths of Caracalla, attacking Porta San Paolo from behind. Self-propelled guns da 47/32, probably from the "Genova Cavalleria" counter-attacked decisively at the Passeggiata Archeologica and at the obelisk of Axum, sacrificing themselves to try to close that dangerous breach. The "Montebello" Regiment, having lost almost all of its armored vehicles in valiant counterattacks, was forced to fall back and its failure was the beginning of the end of the resistance, with the extreme offshoots of the defense falling back towards the barracks of Santa Croce and Macao. The Germans were able to break through the defense of Porta San Paolo only in the afternoon, putting an end to one of the most dramatic and heroic episodes of the Resistance, while the young second lieutenant Vincenzo Fioritto, an officer of the 4th Tankers Regiment, born in Parioli, was trying to make an extreme attempt of resistance. With a platoon of 11 tanks he had gone in the morning to the Ostiense area, to oppose the advance of the German paratroopers in the area of Porta San Paolo. Around 15:30, the tank of Lieutenant Fioritto, preceded by the one piloted by Corporal Baldinotti, slowly went down viale Baccelli, just above the Baths of Caracalla, sent in reconnaissance, because there was the suspicion that on that side there were enemy nuclei: in fact, while the German troops were proceeding from the south (Ostiense area), a Fallschirmjäger unit had moved behind the Italian line. Baldinotti spotted an 88 mm cannon and some 37 mm antitank guns lurking

---

32 *"Commander of a 75-18 self-propelled squadron, in many risky fights against overwhelming forces in terms of number and armament, he exposed himself where the danger was the greatest to animate, encourage and direct his lancers in the attack manoeuvres, made more daring by the impervious and difficult terrain. In charge of protecting with his squadron the retreat of other units, he fought against the enemy on the ground palm to palm, stemming their impetuosity and weakening their boldness. When he arrived near Porta San Paolo, the last bulwark for the defence of the capital, in a fit of rage and rebellion against the fatal outcome of the unequal fight, as if to challenge the enemy from whom he did not feel defeated, he threw himself with his cart and at the head of his squadron against the pressing enemy formations, renewing in an epic charge the glorious traditions of the Italian cavalry. When his chariot was torn apart by an enemy grenade and he himself was mortally wounded, he refused any help offered by his lancers, exclaiming: "Don't touch me, leave me here in my place of honor. Energetic and tenacious character of knight and commander, example of the highest military value. - Rome, Porta San Paolo, September 10, 1943".*

33 *"He participated with the M tank company in combat against the Germans. Received the order to send one of his platoons on reconnaissance, he claimed for himself the honour of being at the head of his tanks and was the first to make contact with the enemy, whose violent reaction of artillerymen struck and immobilized his vehicle, putting his crew out of action and wounding himself. He did not desist from the fight until a new shot reached him in the chest, cutting short his noble life. Beautiful example of heroism, of serene contempt for danger and of high military virtues. - Rome, Porta San Paolo, September 10, 1943".*

in the brushwood, stopped the tank and opened fire. The German reaction was fatal: the paratroopers let the two tanks get closer to target them with their small but effective guns and the two M13/40s were hit by an inferno of fire, which went through the metal sheets like butter. During the fight, Enzo Fioritto was hit by a grenade in the left arm, dying shortly after having exhorted his men to persist in the battle. The tank of Corporal Bruno Baldinotti, who was only 18 years old, was hit by a total of 14 cannon shots and caught fire, but Baldinotti managed to get his commander out of the burning[34] tank. Inside the tank there was also Corporal Carlo Lazzerini, and, despite the fact that they were both wounded, he and Baldinotti continued to fire, managing to eliminate two positions of 37mm antitank guns, but the flames that enveloped the M13/40 caused the death of the two young men[35]. At the end of the battle a strange calm fell over the area and a child unconsciously approached Baldinotti's tank, looking out of the side door, probably left open by the tank leader, seeing the body of young Bruno Baldinotti slumped in the driver's seat. Seeing some German soldiers approaching, the young boy hid and managed to see one of the German soldiers throw a hand grenade inside the M13 still smoking: for this reason, no trace of the body of the young tank driver of the 4th Regiment was found. Enzo Fioritto was awarded the Gold Medal for Military Valor[36], Bruno Baldinotti was awarded the Silver Medal for Military Valor [37]and Carlo Lazzerini was awarded the Bronze Medal for Military Valor[38]. The Training Battalion of the 4th Infantry Carrier Regiment had thus immolated all of its five M13/40 tanks in the clashes of 10 September 1943.

Meanwhile, in the city center, German soldiers supported by an armored vehicle, driving up Via Cavour, were confronted by two AB41 armored cars of the Italian African Police. The

34 Bruno Baldinotti lived in the populous Celio district, 500 meters as the crow flies from the place where he fell in combat: his family knew that he would be mobilized in the area that day.

35 With these simple, yet touching words, Anna Baldinotti remembered her brother's sacrifice: *"Not everyone escaped, my brother Bruno died shooting at the Germans. Not all the Italian army abandoned Rome to the Germans. There were also those who, like my brother, tank driver Bruno Baldinotti, faced the Germans and died. They were few, they were left alone, but they fought…".* At the end of the clashes, his sister Adriana went into the burnt carcass of Baldinotti's wagon, to recover some memories of the fallen young man, but the body had been torn apart by the flames and by the explosion of the hand grenade thrown by a German soldier inside the wagon and the young sister could only collect in a cloth three coins, a spoon, Bruno's gamella and some shells.

36 This is the motivation of the Medal to Enzo Fioritto: *"Commander of a tank platoon M., received the order to attack a strong German column, supported by tanks and powerful artillery, although he was sure that the difficult task would have involved the destruction of his modest means, he faced it with stoic firmness, succeeding at first, operating with extreme audacity, to stop the irruption of the enemy and destroying some anti-tank pieces. When the fight became bitter again and almost all the personnel and the means were useless, with his tank hit several times, operated by him and by the pilot only, he gathered the few surviving tanks and at the head of them he threw himself again on the adversary in a desperate attempt to interdict the way to the Eternal City. Hit by a grenade that removed his left arm, he still found the strength, before breathing his last breath, to incite his handful of heroes to continue the fight. A very young officer, in a short period of general bewilderment, he showed the most, with the extreme sacrifice, the way of duty and honor. - Rome, September 10, 1943".*

37 Baldinotti was initially awarded the Bronze Medal: it seems that the official report on the event was rather "hasty", but, following some testimonies of civilians, the appeal was accepted and the honor changed to Silver Medal two years after the end of the war. This is the motivation, which offers a reconstruction of the fight in part wrong: *"Pilot of tank M participated in fighting against the Germans, demonstrating serenity and contempt for danger. Sent in offensive reconnaissance for which he offered himself voluntarily, even knowing the danger to which he was exposed, he pushed with all the ardor of his youth against the enemy preponderant for forces and means. Hit a first time, he did not give up his noble impulse, succeeding in identifying and destroying two 37mm pieces. Wounded again, he gathered his remaining forces in a supreme effort and managed to get his commander out of the burning tank where he sacrificed his flourishing life. Shining example of preclinary military virtues. - Rome, Porta S. Paolo September 10, 1943".*

38 *"Servant of a tank "M" participated in fighting against the Germans. Having the tank immobilized by the precise fire of the anti-tank pieces of the adversaries, he didn't give up the fight even if wounded, doing his best with enthusiasm and serene disregard of the danger until a new shot didn't destroy his noble existence. - Rome, Porta S. Paolo September 10, 1943".*

latter, despite the unfavorable situation for them, accepted the clash, being both hit and set on fire and the crews died in the flames.

A bitter fight took place also around piazzale Ostiense and along the homonymous avenue, where the 2nd Company of the 12th Battalion of the "Sassari" Division, a platoon of the 5th Squadron of the "Lancieri di Montebello" of the armored Division "Ariete" and some vehicles of the 4th Tankers Regiment spent themselves without economy in a desperate attempt of counterattack. The 5th Squadron Self-propelled guns da 47/32 of the Reggimento "Lancieri di Montebello" was commanded by Captain Camillo Sabatini, who had succeeded the previous day to conquer a German stronghold at the gates of Rome, held by paratroopers superior in number and armament. The 5th Squadron held the position for the entire day, then had to retreat along the Via Ostiense to Porta San Paolo, the last line established for the defense of Rome, where Captain Sabatini found death. Sabatini led an offensive against the Germans with a handful of self-propelled guns, unfortunately without success. Seriously wounded by a machine gun burst, he persisted in remaining at his fighting post, continuing to give orders to his men, until, lifeless, he collapsed to the ground: for his heroic behavior he was decorated with the Gold Medal of Military Valor[39]. Three M13/40 tanks of the Training Battalion of the 4th Tanker Infantry Regiment tried to break through the German line on Via Ostiense, while they were supporting an attack attempt of the 151st Regiment "Sassari" Battalion. They were the tanks that came closest to the line held by the Germans, probably because they entered Via Ostiense from Via del Commercio. They all sacrificed themselves, stopped by the enemy fire. Tank drivers Primo Dall'Occhio and Livio Concin died and tank drivers Aldo Bufano and Antonio D'Agostino were burnt in the fire of their tank. On the via Ostiense the German paratroopers gave a demonstration of great determination and combativeness, resulting precise and deadly in the counter tank shooting, nailing, one after the other, the Italian tanks and self-propelled guns, that tried to stop the enemy advance. In fact, even though they were without armored vehicles, since their eleven Marder self-propelled guns had remained in Frascati for the defense of the German commands, the paratroopers of the 2. Fallschirmjäger-Division were able to inflict terrible losses to the Italians, thanks to a wise use of the anti-tank weapons they had in their equipment.

As we have seen, already in the morning, in order to diminish the pressure on the "Granatieri", around 7:00 a.m. General Carboni had ordered the Division "Ariete II" to prepare a rapid column from Tivoli to Via Tiburtina[40]. The column of the "Ariete" was composed as follows: Division Tactical Command, a formation unit including all available armored cars, a self-propelled group of the Regiment "Lucca", a self-propelled Squadron of the Regiment "Vittorio Emanuele II", the 18th Bersaglieri Regiment, which had passed to the Division a

---

39 *"Commander of a 47/32 self-propelled squadron, overcoming obstacles in a terrain strongly beaten by enemy mortars, he contributed to the action that led to the conquest of an essential stronghold against German paratroopers superior in number and weapons. Once the stronghold was conquered, he kept it and garrisoned it despite the insufficiency of the available firepower, hanging on to it for a whole day, with the awareness of contributing to a stronger resistance of the troops operating in the sector. Aware since the beginning of the ineluctability of the sacrifice, he fell back contending the ground inch by inch until, arrived at the last line established for the defense of Rome, he led his self-propelled vehicles in a desperate attack against the overwhelming enemy, renewing in a supreme charge the glories of the ancient cavalry. Wounded, he remained at his post heartening his fighters, then stoically expired with the pride of his duty offering his life in holocaust to the Homeland. Shining example of heroism and high military virtues - Rome, Via Ostiense - Porta S. Paolo, 9 - 10 September 1943.*
40 At the same time, the Division "Piave" received orders to converge on Rome by 4 p.m. and to stand at the gates of the city.

few hours before. Subsequently, when Lieutenant Colonel Giaccone went to meet the units, it was specified to form two columns to start for the streets of Lunghezza and Settecamini, in order to take the Germans behind on the Appia. General Cadorna, commander of the Division "Ariete II" hesitated and the columns were actually prepared only around 3 p.m. by the vice-commander general Dardano Fenulli: the first one was constituted by the Group "Lucca" and by a self-propelled Squadron of the Regiment "Vittorio Emanuele II", the second one by the 18th R.E.Co. of the Bersaglieri. They finally reached contact with the Germans at Ciampino, after having already defeated some enemy nuclei, around 19:30 the two columns were stopped by the effective cessation of hostilities and recalled by General Cadorna.

Taking a brief step back, let's review in detail the events that occurred to the 18th Bersaglieri Regiment. In the night between September 9 and 10 the unit had been dispatched to protect the roads leading from Palestrina to Tivoli and in the early morning hours had clashes with the Germans, during which was wounded Lieutenant Mazzoni, commander of the 2nd Tank Company L6/40. The Regiment, passed to the "Ariete II" Division and returned to Settecamini, marched to deploy its Companies to the left of the Italian device between Porta San Sebastiano, the Archaeological walk and Porta San Paolo. Around 17:00 the column of the 18th Bersaglieri Regiment came into contact with a German roadblock, armed with 88mm cannons, whose commander informed the Italians that a cease-fire agreement had been in effect for an hour. According to another version, at 17:00 the unit was informed, by means of leaflets launched to a Cicogna aircraft, that a cease-fire had been in effect since 16:00. The column therefore returned to Settecamini, where, after a German air attack conducted by JU87, the unit, whose commander was wounded, disbanded and surrendered to German MPs, after having sabotaged a good part of its own means.

One of the last battles of the day is recounted by Carlo Bonciani in his famous book "*Squadron F*" published three years after those terrible days and the narration perfectly conveys the state of confusion that reigned in those moments, characterized by hysterical attempts to resist the enemy. Bonciani commanded a nucleus of about fifty paratroopers of the X Arditi Regiment: "*Anyway, to protect ourselves, let me move forward with my men. I'm going to occupy the buildings of E42. From up there you can control every movement very well and they want to dislodge us! We need two battalions. The colonel[41] says no. He says no again. The order is to keep on that line. I try to make him understand that we can't see anything from there.... Let's at least get some armor out. He replies annoyed.*

*The wake-up call, shortly after five o'clock, was abrupt: we were caught under an inferno of fire; they were pulling especially from the E42 area. The colonel shouts at me, "You were right; it could have been us up there!" Good sucker! I don't answer him, it's useless anyway. I gather my men, to the hand under the viaduct, from where we respond as best we can to the fire. The trouble is that you can't pinpoint exactly where they're shooting from. It's all a vast semicircle that seems to be slowly closing in around us. We throw away the shots. We start to aim in the direction of the E42. With us are Castelbarco (captain of the "Montebello") and the vice-commander of the "Montebello". What a fine officer! He fell wounded after only a hundred meters; in the chest.*

---

41 He is Colonel Giordani, commander of the R.E.Co. "Montebello".

*"Go ahead, don't worry about me," he orders me.*

*But we don't get very far; they're throwing a rain of mortars at us: luckily they're shooting badly, but I already have three wounded. We go up another fifty yards. Now they're shooting with heavy machine guns... It is impossible to continue. But we've pinpointed their firing positions and I send a man down with a note for the colonel: I've made a sort of sketch and I'm showing him where they're firing from, let's hope he can figure it out! I asked him to get the tanks out. In the meantime we take cover as best we can without ceasing to return fire; then we attempt an attack, but they throw us back down with hand grenades. We couldn't use them because of the steep slope: they would fall on us; too bad! Perhaps we would have made it. Three armored cars come out from under the flyover and immediately start an accelerated firing; I can see that the Colonel has understood why they are aiming right. It's a good time to retreat. I reach the colonel. He comes back screaming like a beast shot to death, an officer of the three armored cars that came out: burn! We throw blankets at him. The cars have been hit, he manages to say; the road doesn't allow for any movement and all three are on fire like haystacks"[42].*

During the fighting to defend the city, and especially during the clashes at Porta San Paolo, many civilians spontaneously and in a more or less organized manner, flanked the Italian troops, fighting even to the extreme sacrifice. We remember, because directly involved with the events of the tank divisions engaged in the defense of the Capital, the contribution of the twenty-four years old Carla Capponi. On September 9, she joined a group of poorly armed civilians who were guarding the Basilica of San Paolo, doing their best all day and all night to assist the wounded who were being concentrated around the religious building. On September 10, Carla Capponi found herself at Porta San Paolo and did not abandon the line of fire, although unarmed. While she was retreating at the end of the fighting towards the archaeological promenade, she witnessed an Italian tank retreating near Porta Capena being machine-gunned by a German Tiger. Without fear, he jumped on the Italian tank and managed to drag a tank driver out of the turret, saving his life by carrying him to his home. Not far away, in Via Gioberti, the fourteen-year-old student Carlo Del Papa lost his life in a similar action, while he was trying to defend an armored car. The armored car was firing towards a building where a group of Germans had barricaded themselves and were attempting to eliminate the armored car with a dense launch of hand grenades and machine gun fire. Carlo, in the middle of the street, was hit by a volley of bullets: he was the youngest casualty of the tragic days of Rome.

---

42 Bonciani Carlo, "Squadron F," work cited in bibliography.

▲ The crew of an M42 self-propelled 75/18 "Montebello" waiting for the German advance.

▼ Porta San Paolo and the Cestia Pyramid in a vintage postcard.

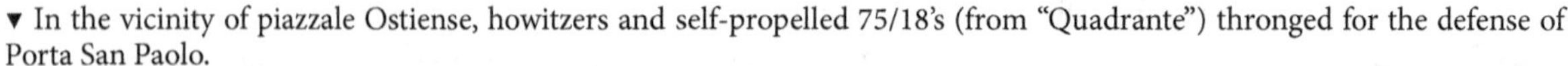

▲ A group of soldiers, probably from the "Granatieri" Division, are stationed in front of the Pyramid Cestia. Further on, near Porta San Paolo, a truck, perhaps a Bianchi Miles, and a self-propelled vehicle (Pisanò) can be seen.

▼ In the vicinity of piazzale Ostiense, howitzers and self-propelled 75/18's (from "Quadrante") thronged for the defense of Porta San Paolo.

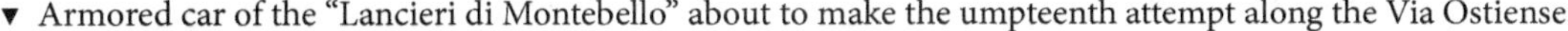

▲ The 100/17 howitzers of the "Sassari" Division on Piazzale Ostiense: on the right is the Roma - Lido station, with the terminus of the tramway line (Pisanò).

▼ Armored car of the "Lancieri di Montebello" about to make the umpteenth attempt along the Via Ostiense.

▲ Behind the pieces of the "Sassari", with their respective ammunition wagons, you can see, in the background on the left, the train station, inaugurated in May 1938 for Hitler's visit to Rome, while on the right the gazometro, a tank once used for the storage of "city gas", a mixture of gas derived from coal used for public lighting (Pisanò).

▼ Figurative representation of the death at Porta San Paolo of Captain Romolo Fugazza, commander of Squadron of Semoventi da 75/18 of the 8th Regiment "Lancieri di Montebello".

▲ The lieutenant of the Lancieri di "Montebello" Silvano Gray de Cristoforis, who lost his life hit by a grenade on September 10 at Porta San Paolo, where a memorial stone remembers him. The previous day he had written a four-page letter to his family saying goodbye, convinced that he would never return home, a letter of farewell to life, which he knew he would have sacrificed for the honor of Italy.  He went to the attack carrying on his turret the flag of the Regiment and the heraldic flag of his noble family. In 1948, the Minister of Defense, Cipriano Facchinetti, awarded Silvano Gray De Cristoforis the Silver Medal for Military Valor.

▲ A crude pictorial depiction of the Battle of St. Paul's Gate.

▲ Iconic image of the sacrifice of the Regiment "Lancieri di Montebello" during the defense of Rome.

▼ The marble plaque placed at Porta San Paolo by the City of Rome on September 10, 1970 in memory of the battles sustained by the soldiers of the Royal Army against the German armed forces. The inscription reads: *"To the resistance that heroically marked here on September 10, 1943 the second Risorgimento"*.

▲ German paratroopers are preparing to battery a PaK40 on the morning of September 10, 1943 in Via Ostiense in front of the Officine del Gas.

▼ Inverted triangle formation of the 2. Fallschirmjäger-Division's anti-tank unit in front of the General Markets.

# THE END OF THE CLASHES

After the fall of Porta San Paolo, the Germans infiltrated the city without the possibility, by now, of being stopped, since there was not even a semblance of organic resistance. However, numerous small clashes developed, in which both civilians and soldiers were protagonists. While they were trying to retreat towards their headquarters, some trucks of the 4th Tank Regiment were stopped by an officer of the Grenadier Guards in Piazza Venezia; the officer ordered to defend Via dell'Impero (today Via dei Fori Imperiali), but since the Germans were not coming, the crews of the trucks decided to march along Via Cavour to Termini Station. Here, at the Hotel Continental, a group of German soldiers, besieged by Italian soldiers and civilians, defended themselves strenuously with intense rifle fire and hand grenades. Clashes also took place in Via Gioberti, but total confusion reigned, as these were the last outbreaks of senseless resistance in the city. Piazza dell'Esedra had been transformed into a sort of field hospital, overflowing with wounded. Due to the absence of an articulated plan for the defense of the city, Rome capitulated quickly, despite the heroic acts of the troops of the Royal Army and civilians. The last fighting took place at the Passeggiata Archeologica, while units of the "Ariete II" Divisions tried in vain to reach the theater of the clashes.

In the rest of Rome there was a strange atmosphere as described by Paolo Monelli: *"Indifferent to the appeals of the anti-fascists, the population of Rome maintained its imperturbable calm. The Romans distinctly heard the cannon shots, knew that there was fighting in many suburbs, saw the wounded brought to safety; but they waited for the end of the battle, probably convinced that it was already lost and certain, in any case, that they could do nothing to change its fate. In the center of the city, even where the German shells had fallen, an absurdly casual atmosphere reigned. At Porta San Giovanni, the A.T.A.G.'s trammen barricaded the doorways with the cars present in the square and with buses placed sideways. The fighting moved towards Termini Station where a train with twenty-two cars was stationed and which constituted the mobile command of the S.M.R.E.; the detachment that defended it was commanded by Major Carlo Benedetti who, with 13 soldiers and numerous civilians, railway workers and simple citizens, defended the convoy standing on the third track. At the head of the train a 20mm machine gun was placed, another one under the canopy of Via Marsala, which soon fell into the hands of the Germans. At 20:30 everything was over with the death of 6 soldiers and 41 civilians, of which 8 were unknown. With the conclusion of this clash there were no more military units with a minimum of organization able to face the Germans. Some shots were heard for some time, a German motorcyclist was killed in Via del Tritone, in front of the headquarters of the newspaper "Il Popolo d'Italia", then total silence fell. People began to go out again, in defiance of the curfew, which no authority, evidently, was able to enforce that evening. Berlin issued a radio communiqué announcing triumphantly that the German army had conquered Rome without encountering any notable resistance.*

It is very difficult to calculate the losses of these days of last and desperate defense, even if the most reliable figure for the dead is 1,167, of which more than 200 civilians (according to some sources 400). General Mario Capitani, Chief of Staff of the Rome Army Corps in 1943, in his book "La difesa di Roma" (The Defence of Rome) gives a higher figure for the military alone[43]: the military dead were 609 (19 officers and 590 NCOs and soldiers), the missing 753 (41 officers and 712 NCOs and soldiers), the wounded 558 (11 officers and 547 NCOs and soldiers). The number of armored vehicles destroyed during the fighting was 15, 5 M tanks, 4 L tanks and 6 self-propelled 47/32 tanks. The Germans declared to have lost, in the course of the battle for Rome, a hundred men between dead and wounded, 1 88 cannon and other 2 artillery pieces, besides having brought back damages to 3 assault cannons and 2 tanks.

At 4 p.m. on September 10, Lieutenant Colonel Leandro Giaccone, on behalf of General Giorgio Carlo Calvi di Bergolo, in the villa in Frascati where Field Marshal Kesselring's (OBS) command was based, signed with General Westphal the document "Surrender of Rome", previously approved by Marshal Enrico Caviglia of Italy[44]. Rome should have remained "Open City", but the next day Kesserling declared that Rome was part of the war territory and, consequently, was subject to the German code of war. All Italian units were disarmed and disbanded[45], with the exception of an aliquot of the "Piave" Division, which had to guarantee public order together with the soldiers of the P.A.I.; the soldiers of the "Piave" were however disarmed on September 23, 1943, after the proclamation of the Italian Social Republic.

On September 11, the command of the Armored Corps, now existing only on paper, due to the dissolution of the units, was entrusted to General Raffaele Cadorna, commander of the Division "Ariete II", who gave himself away to join the Clandestine Military Front, which was being organized under the leadership of Colonel Giuseppe Cordero Lanza di Montezemolo.

The main part of the 10th Regiment "Lancieri di Vittorio Emanuele II" did not take part in the fights in the city, with the exception, as we have seen, of the 6th Squadron of the 2nd Group and the 8th Self-propelled Squadron of the 3rd Group, since it was stationed between Anguillara, on the Bracciano lake, and Osteria Nuova. Its numerous tanks (about 350 tanks, self-propelled and command tanks) were neatly assembled in the plain of Ponte Lucano, near Tivoli, after the "cease-fire", where the Regiment remained compact during the negotiations for the establishment of "Roma Città Aperta" and for the disarmament of the Italian troops. The commander, Colonel Guido Raby, made an attempt at the Divisional Command, offering to take only with the tanks and self-propelled guns in Abruzzo, where he would refuel at the airfield of Pescara, but the Command suggested to the Colonel to desist from this enterprise, which could cause reprisals not only on the unit, but also on the Roman citizens. The Colonel then ordered to distribute all existing escorts to the Lancers and delivered to each one this statement signed by him, which released them from any commitment:

"*Armored Regiment Lancieri Vittorio Emanuele II, Command. P.M. 160 - September 12, 1943*

*I declare that the.... has remained in my Regiment and has entirely fulfilled his duty until the moment in which I have given him peremptory orders to consider himself at liberty.*

*Lieutenant Colonel Commander of the Guido Raby Regiment.*"

On September 13th all the Regiment's vehicles were handed over intact to the Germans, who

---

43 Page 106, work cited in bibliography.
44 On September 13, during a meeting with Field Marshal Kesserling, Enrico Caviglia said: "*You see how Italy is reduced: like Christ at the column. Everyone can spit on it or slap it and beat it*".
45 The "Ram II" Division was declared dissolved on September 16.

used them to reinforce their units in Italy and in the Balkans, after having scrupulously inventoried them. Representing the General Staff of the Armored Corps was Colonel Menotti Chieli, while for the Division "Ariete II" Colonel Carlo Salinari Chief of Staff, who formally replaced the commander General Cadorna, who had gone underground.

On the morning of September 17, a column of vehicles brought the officers of the "Lancieri di Vittorio Emanuele II" to Rome[46], carrying the Regiment's standard, which was placed in Castel Sant'Angelo. Before leaving Tivoli, Colonel Raby had given the regimental drapes to the senior officers and captains, who committed themselves with a written declaration to keep them as relics and to give them back in case of reconstitution of the Regiment. A dismounted group of soldiers of the Regiment later participated in the war of liberation in the area of Garigliano.

The CXXXV Battalion of Self-Propelled Tanks, equipped with 75/34 M42 self-propelled guns and positioned at Cesano, also took practically no part in any battle.

On September 13, the 136th Armored Division "Centauro II" was also disarmed. The Armistice of September 8 had produced a great impression in the divisions of the Division; in the afternoon of September 9 Captain Hans Schacht, member of the General Staff of the 11. Fliegerkorps of General Kurt Student had a conversation with Lieutenant Colonel Leandro Giaccone, during which he transmitted a message of Student, addressed to General Calvi di Bergolo: "[...] *everything possible will be done to avoid contact with the Division "M" until, in a short time, the Germans will be uncontested masters of Rome. General Student also communicates to General Calvi that, if it will be possible to avoid fighting with the division "Centauro", its components in consideration of their state of mind, will not be taken prisoner in Germany, but sent free with the honor of arms"*. After having received news of the agreement of "cease fire" on September 10th, the Division remained on its positions, uncertain on what to do, and in the afternoon the order to disarm and to deliver all the materials to the Germans arrived, but the unit remained in arms (the only unit in this privileged condition) until September 12th when some emissAriete of the 11. Fliegerkorps reached the units of the "Centauro", proposing to continue to fight under German orders, swearing loyalty to Hitler. This fact, united to the arrival of the news of the liberation of Mussolini to the Gran Sasso, marked the definitive collapse of the Division. Part of the effects abandoned the position, others tried to remain, in that atmosphere of confusion that characterized those terrible days. On the 13th of September all the materials supplied by the Wehrmacht, tanks, armored vehicles, self-propelled guns, cannons and vehicles, were delivered in an atmosphere of absolute calm to German units, to be subsequently used on the front of Anzio and Cassino. It was the end of the 1st Armored Legionary Division "M", but 3 officers and about sixty legionnaires decided to continue the war on the side of the now ex-German allies and on September 16 went to form the embryo of what would later become the Armored Group "Leonessa" of the Republican National Guard, used in the anti-partisan fight between Lombardy, Piedmont and Emilia-Romagna. Before being transferred to the Brescia area, the "Tankers" in black shirts garrisoned the headquarters of the reconstituted Roman Fascio in Piazza Colonna in Rome between September 17 and 18, 1943, is documented by photographs of some M13/40 tanks and Camionette Desertiche model 43, taken from the warehouses of the 4th Tankers Regiment.

---

46 The Germans had allowed officers to keep their service pistols.

▲ The E.I.A.R. Radio Station at Prato Smeraldo, manned by the 2nd Battery of the DCI Self-propelled Group.

► Captain Nunzio Incannamorte, commander of the 2nd Battery of the DCI Semoventi Group, lost his life while protecting the Radio Station of Prato Smeraldo.

▲ Corporal Bruno Baldinotti and Corporal Carlo Lazzerini of the 4th Carristi Regiment.

▲ Enzo Fioritto's M13/30 tank, at the bottom right the tank of the young Bruno Baldinotti, both hit by German anti-tank guns on September 10 in Viale Baccelli. On the right you can see a little girl: she is Adriana, Bruno Baldinotti's sister.

▼ The M13/40 tank of Corporal Bruno Baldinotti and Corporal Carlo Lazzerini, in Via Baccelli, next to the Baths of Caracalla. In the background that of Second Lieutenant Enzo Fioritto: it is not clear why it was facing the opposite side of Baldinotti's, as if it was trying to regain the position from which it had come.

▲ The memorial stone placed on Viale Baccelli remembers both the two young tank drivers Bruno Baldinotti and Corporal Carlo Lazzerini who died on September 10, 1943.

▼ Lieutenant Enzo Fioritto, Gold Medal for Military Valor in memory. On the right the plaque dedicated to Enzo Fioritto at the Archaeological Walk. The two plaques, the one dedicated to Fioritto and the other to Baldinotti and Lazzerini, are placed at the sides of the road, exactly in the position where the wrecks of the two tanks were found at the end of the clashes.

▲ Fioritto's M13/40 tank marked "RE 2810" next to the remains of the Baths of Caracalla.

▼ Another image of Lieutenant Fioritto's tank, taken from the back: you can see the damage caused by the flames on the back of the tank.

▲ Captain Camillo Sabatini, commander of the 5th Squadron Semoventi da 47/32 of the Regiment "Lancieri di Montebello", fallen in the Capital on September 10, 1943, decorated with Gold Medal for Military Valor.

▲ Officers of the "Sassari" Division are taken by motorcycle to the tactical command of the 2. Fallschirmjäger-Division to communicate the surrender of the troops defending Porta San Paolo (B.A.).

▼ The officers are accompanied blindfolded to the officers of the German paratroopers. The tactical command post of the German paratroopers had been set up in a meadow behind the Mercati Generali in the Ostiense area. In the background you can see the river port of Rome, once a docking station for the transport of goods within the capital. The area of the clashes (Porta San Paolo, Piazzale Ostiense, the Pyramid) was adjacent to the industrial area of Rome, where there was also the municipal slaughterhouse, the OMI (Ottica Meccanica Italiana), the Vasca Navale Nazionale (a basin for testing boats, now the headquarters of the University of Roma Tre) and a cement factory (B.A.).

▲ The Italian officers are disbanded: the face of the Grenadier expresses a pride and determination, despite the dramatic situation for the Italian military (B.A.).

▼ An officer of the Alpine Artillery (B.A.) also participated in the negotiations during which the terms of the delivery of the weapons were discussed.

▲ The faces of the Italian officers are eloquently tense, due to the dramatic moment they are experiencing (B.A.).

▼ A German armored car in Rome in September 1943 (B.A.).

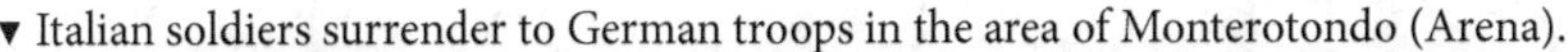

▲ Machine gun nest of paratroopers of the 2. Fallschirmjäger-Division (B.A.)

▼ Italian soldiers surrender to German troops in the area of Monterotondo (Arena).

▲ At the end of the clashes in the Capital, some German paratroopers with Italian prisoners taken at EUR (Arena).

▼ The sad remains of the Italian artillery at the end of the battles at Porta San Paolo: abandoned cannons, empty ammunition boxes, equipment scattered everywhere. The battle for Rome is definitely over (Pisanò).

▲ Some civilians wander among the pieces abandoned by the "Sassari" on Piazzale Ostiense. The photograph, taken on the morning of September 11, can be easily compared with one of the previous photographs, taken in practically the same position (Pisanò).

▼ Another sad image of a Skoda howitzer abandoned together with its ammunition wagon near the Ostiense Station at Porta San Paolo (Pisanò).

▲ Italian equipment abandoned at the end of the clashes behind the office of the Regie Poste behind Porta San Paolo, next to the Ostiense Station: the firearms are Austrian war surplus of the First World War.

▼ Life resumes and the population of Rome returns to walk the streets that, until a few hours before, had been the scene of terrible fighting between Italians and Germans. It is curious how, right in the middle of the science, there is an Italian soldier marching, with his rucksack slung over his shoulder, without fear of encountering enemy soldiers.

▲ A 47/32 L40 self-propelled vehicle, probably belonging to the "Genova Cavalry" Regiment, in front of the Stele of Axum: the vehicle was gutted by enemy shots (Manes).

▲ The same self-propelled vehicle on the previous page seen from another perspective (Manes).

▼ The wreckage of one of the self-propelled M42 75/18, plate number "RE 6225", of the 5th Squadron of the II Gruppo dei "Lancieri di Montebello", commanded by Captain Romolo Fugazza (Manes).

▲ The same M42 self-propelled 75/18 of the "Montebello" photographed from the opposite side. Captain Fugazza's unit attempted a charge towards the German anti-tank guns along the Via Ostiense (B.A.).

▲ A close-up picture of the casemate of the self-propelled vehicle bearing the license plate "RE 6225", showing the damage produced by an enemy anti-tank shot on the top of the vehicle and, on the left, next to the fire mouth, the symbol of the department (Manes).

▼ A German crawler Sd.Kfz. 2 kleines Kettenkrad, used to pull anti-tank pieces, reduced to scrap on the Via Ostiense. In the distance, on the right, there is an immobilized Italian tank (Manes).

▲ Another Italian armored car in Via della Stazione Ostiense, where, just in the days of the clashes, there were works of resurfacing, as you can see on the right of the picture.

▼ In the foreground, to the left of the self-propelled vehicle, there is a cart with a cistern, probably used to transport road bitumen.

▲ Close-up of the self-propelled vehicle from the previous images, seen from a different perspective.

▼ M13/40 tanks of the 4th Carristi Regiment on the Via Ostiense stopped by German fire on 10 September 1943. On the left the tank marked "RE 3414", on board of which Primo Dall'Occhio and Livio Concin died, while on the right the tank "RE 3048", on which the tank drivers Aldo Bufano and Antonio D'Agostino (Manes) burned.

▲ These two M13/40s, which were probably supporting an attempted attack by a battalion of the 151st "Sassari" Regiment, were the armored vehicles that came closest to the German positions. In front of the tanks the twisted remains of an Italian TL37 artillery tractor (NARA).

▼ The two M13 tanks are located on the stretch of Via Ostiense at the end of the square of the former gazometro, not far from the Mercati Generali. Once the fighting was over, people of all ages wanted to get closer to the armored cars (NARA).

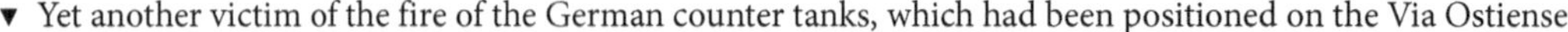

▲ Once the fighting was over, civilians approached the abandoned Italian armored vehicles in the streets of Rome with curiosity.

▼ Yet another victim of the fire of the German counter tanks, which had been positioned on the Via Ostiense.

▲ An image probably taken a few days after the surrender of the Italian armed forces in Rome: a group of kids having fun on a 47/32 self-propelled gun near the Cestia pyramid (Manes).

▲ Remains of a 47/32 self-propelled gun burned in front of the building, then under construction, of the present F.A.O., near the Archaeological Promenade. This and three other self-propelled vehicles were hit during the skilful encirclement maneuver carried out by the Fallschirmjäger anti-tank units.

▼ Another Italian 75/18 self-propelled vehicle blocked by the fire of German anti-tank vehicles positioned on Via Ostiense near the Mercati Generali.

▲ Wreck of a 47/32 L40 self-propelled aircraft of the 5th Self-propelled Squadron of the Regiment "Lancieri di Montebello", commanded by Captain Camillo Sabatini.

▼ Jubilant German soldiers aboard an Italian light wagon pass in front of the Aquarium in Piazza Manfredo Fanti in Rome.

▲ After having fought practically uninterruptedly for two days, for the Italian soldiers the moment of surrender to the German paratroopers had arrived: in Via Asmara a group of soldiers of the "Piave" Division were rounded up without putting up any resistance.

▲ Colonel Leandro Giaccone confers with General Westphal, Kesserling's chief of staff, in Frascati, to discuss ways to cease fire the Italian troops in the capital (Arena).

▼ Once the clashes in Rome were over, a long column of Italian soldiers, headed for captivity, marched near a group of German paratroopers, indifferent to the defeated soldiers (B.A.).

▲ Two German armored cars Sd.Kfz 231 8 rad in Via di Santa Costanza directed towards Piazza Istria in Rome in the days following the clashes for the defense of the Capital (B.A.).

▼ German self-propelled vehicles on the streets of Rome, after the cease-fire agreed upon with the Italian military authorities (Arena).

▲ Concentrated and loaded onto trucks, the militiamen of the Regio Esercito were sent toward captivity, a scene that would be repeated throughout Italy and in every theater where Italian soldiers were located (Pisanò).

# BIBLIOGRAPHY

## BOOKS


- AA.VV., "Storia dei mezzi corazzati", Fratelli Fabbri Editori, Milano 1976.
- AA.VV., "Soldati e Battaglie della Seconda Guerra Mondiale", Hobby & Work Italiana Editrice, Bresso (MI), 1999.
- Arena Nino, "R.S.I. – Forze Armate della Repubblica Sociale – La guerra in Italia – 1943", Ermanno Albertelli Editore, Parma, 2002.
- Barba Selene, "La Resistenza dei militari italiani all'Estero – Francia e Corsica", Rivista militare, Roma, 1995.
- Barlozzetti Ugo, Pirella Alberto, "Mezzi dell'Esercito italiano 1935 – 1945", Editoriale Olimpia, Firenze, 1986.
- Benvenuti Bruno, Colonna Ugo, "Fronte Terra" volumi 1, 2/I, 2/II e 2/III, Edizioni Bizzarri, Roma 1974.
- Bonciani Carlo, "Squadrone F", Vallecchi, Firenze, 1946.
- Capitani Mario, "La difesa di Roma – Cronistoria dal 25 luglio al 29 settembre 1943", Edizioni Stem Mucchi, 1973.
- Cappellano Filippo, Pignato Nicola, "Gli autoveicoli da combattimento dell'Esercito Italiano", volume I, S.M.E. – Ufficio Storico, Roma, 2002.
- Cappellano Filippo, Pignato Nicola, "Gli autoveicoli da combattimento dell'Esercito Italiano", volume II, S.M.E. – Ufficio Storico, Roma, 2002.
- Cappellano Filippo, Pignato Nicola, "Il Regio Esercito alla vigilia dell'8 settembre 1943", Ermanno Albertelli Editore Parma, 2003.
- Carro Giuseppe, Grioni Daniele, "Fortini di Sardegna 1940-1943. Storia di un patrimonio da salvaguardare e valorizzare", Grafica del Parteolla, Dolianova (CA), 2014.
- Cataldi Umberto, Di Nardo Roberto, "La difesa di Roma e i Granatieri di Sardegna nel settembre 1943", Stato Maggiore dell' Esercito, Roma, 1993.
- Ceva Lucio, Curami Andrea, "La meccanizzazione dell'Esercito fino al 1943", S.M.E – Ufficio Storico, Roma, 1989.
- Commissione Italiana di Storia Militare, "La partecipazione delle Forze Armate alla Guerra di Liberazione e di Resistenza – 8 settembre 1943 8 maggio 1945", Ente Editoriale per l'Anna dei Carabinieri, Roma, 2003.
- Corbatti Sergio, Nava Marco, "Come il diamante", Laran Editions, Bruxelles, 2008.
- Crippa Paolo, "I Reparti Corazzati della Repubblica Sociale Italiana 1943 -1945", Marvia Edizioni, Voghera (PV), 2006.
- Crippa Paolo, "I mezzi corazzati italiani della Guerra Civile 43- 45", Mattioli 1885, Fidenza (PR), 2015.
- Crippa Paolo, Manes Luigi, "Italia 43-45 - I mezzi delle Unità cobelligeranti", Mattioli 1885, Fidenza (PR), 2018.
- Crippa Paolo, "I carristi di Mussolini - Il gruppo corazzato "Leonessa" dalla M.V.S.N. alla R.S.I.", Soldiershop, Zanica (BG), 2019.
- Crippa Paolo, Cucut Carlo, "I reparti corazzati italiani nei Balcani 1941-1945", Soldiershop, Zanica (BG), 2019.
- Cucut Carlo, "Le Forze Armate della R.S.I. 1943 – 1945 – Forze di terra", G.M.T., Trento, 2005.
- D'Agostini Lorenzo, Forti Roberto, "Il sole è sorto a Roma", A.N.P.I., Roma, 1965.

- De Lorenzis Ugo, "Dal primo all'ultimo giorno. Ricordi di guerra 1939 - 1945", Longanesi, Milano, 1971.
- Di Giusto Stefano, "Il Gruppo Corazzato San Giusto dal Regio Esercito alla R.S.I. 1934 – 1945", Laran Éditions, Bruxelles, 2008.
- Finazzer Enrico, Caretta Luigi, "Le camionette del Regio Esercito", G.M.T., Trento, 2020.
- Fracassi Claudio, "La battaglia di Roma 1943. I giorni della passione sotto l'occupazione nazista", Mur
- Franceschini Luigi, "50 anni dopo", Associazione Nazionale Granatieri di Sardegna, 1993.
- Girlando Raffaele, "PAI – Polizia dell'Africa Italiana", Italia Editrice, Campobasso, 1996.
- Girlando Raffaele; "Storia della PAI: Polizia dell'Africa Italiana 1936-1945", Italia Editrice New, Foggia, 2003
- Giusti Maria Teresa, Rossi Aga, "Una guerra a parte. I militari italiani nei Balcani, 1940-1945", Il Mulino, Bologna, 2017.
- Guglielmi Daniele, "Italian Armour in German Service 1944 – 1945", Mattioli 1885, Parma, 2005.
- Guglielmi Daniele, Tallillo Andrea, Tallillo Antonio, "Carro L3. Carri veloci, carri leggeri, derivati", GMT, Trento, 2004.
- Guglielmi Daniele, Tallillo Andrea, Tallillo Antonio, "Carro L6 – Carri leggeri, semoventi, derivati", seconda edizione, GMT, Trento, 2019.
- Guglielmi Daniele, Tallillo Andrea, Tallillo Antonio, "Carro M. Carri medi M11/39, M13/40, M14/41, M15/42, semoventi e altri derivati", GMT, Trento, 2010.
- Guglielmi Daniele, Tallillo Andrea, Tallillo Antonio, "Carro M. Carri medi M11/39, M13/40, M14/41, M15/42, semoventi e altri derivati", volume 2, GMT, Trento, 2012.
- Masacci Luca, "I veicoli corazzati italiani 1940 – 1943: album fotografico", Mattioli 1885, Fidenza (PR), 2013.
- Mattesini Francesco, "I combattimenti di Monterosi, lago di Bracciano, Monterotondo e Porta San Paolo", Edito in proprio, Roma, 2020.
- Marzilli Marco, Mori Alessandra, "Roma 1943-1944 ieri & oggi", H.E.-Herald Editore, Roma, 2007.
- Mei Bruno, "I Lancieri di Montebello alla difesa di Roma 8-10 Settembre 1943", Edizioni Corporazione Arti Grafiche, Roma, 1981.
- Meleca Vincenzo, "I carri armati poco conosciuti del Regio Esercito. Prototipi, piccole serie e carri esteri", Associazione Culturale TraccePerLaMeta, Sesto Calende (VA), 2015.
- Monelli Paolo, "Roma 1943", Giulio Einaudi Editore, Torino, 2020.
- Pafi Benedetto, Benvenuti Bruno, "Roma in Guerra - immagini inedite settembre 1943-giungo 1944", Edizioni Oberdan, Roma, 1985.
- Papò Paolo Emilio, "I mezzi corazzati italiani. I primi quarant'anni", IBN Editore, Roma, 2011.
- Parri Maurizio, "Tracce di Cingolo", A.N.C.I., Verona, 2016.
- Parri Maurizio e Bianchi Carlo, "A Nessuno Secondi, le ricompense al valor militare ai Carristi dal 1927 a oggi", A.N.C.I., Roma, 2020.
- Parri Maurizio, "Tributo al 31° Reggimento Carri", Soldiershop Editore, Zanica (BG), 2021.
- Pignato Nicola, "1912 – 1985 Dalla Libia al Libano", Editrice Scorpione, Taranto, 1989.
- Pignato Nicola, "Motori!!! Le truppe corazzate italiane 1919 – 1994", GMT, Trento, 1995.
- Pignato Nicola, "Italian Armored Vehicles of World War Two", Squadron Signal Pub. USA, 2004.

- Pignato Nicola, "Italian Medium Tank in Action", Squadron Signal Piblications, USA, 2001.
- Pignato Nicola, Cappella Filippo, "Insegne, uniformi, distintivi e tradizioni delle truppe corazzate italiane", T&T Editore, Dogana (San Marino), 2005.
- Pignato Nicola, "Un secolo di autoblindate in Italia", Mattioli 1885, Fidenza (PR), 2008.
- Pisanò Giorgio, "Storia della Guerra Civile in Italia", Edizioni F.P.E., Milano, 1965.
- Predoević Dinko, Dimitrijević Bojan, "Oklopne postrojbe Sila Osovine na jugoistoku Europe u Drugome svjetskom ratu", Despot Infinitus d.o.o., Zagabria (Croazia), 2015.
- Ratti Italo Franco, "Con la Centauro, con la Monterosa", memorie edite in proprio.
- Riccio Ralph A., "Italian tanks and combat vehicles of World War II", Mattioli 1885, Fidenza (PR), 2010.
- Solinas Gioachino, "I Granatieri di Sardegna nella difesa di Roma del settembre '43", Gallizzi Editore, Sassari, 1968.
- Tognarini Ivano, Panicucci Massimo, "La battaglia di Piombino", ESI, Napoli, 1999.
- Tullio Saverio, "La difesa di Roma 8-9-10 settembre 1942", Associazione Militari In Congedo – Lazio, 2011.
- Tumiati Gaetano, "Morire per vivere : vita e lettere di Francesco Tumiati Medaglia d'Oro della Resistenza", Corbo, Ferrara, 1995.
- Zangrandi Ruggero, "1943: 25 luglio – 8 settembre", Feltrinelli Editore, Milano, 1964
- Zannoni Mario, "Parma 1943, 8 settembre", Editrice PPS, Parma, 1997.

## ARTICLES

- Cappellano Filippo, "La Divisione Corazzata "M" poi "Centauro II", in "Storia Militare" number 133 - October 2004.
- Degl'Innocenti Carlo, "La battaglia di Piombino", in "L'Unità", September 2, 1074.
- Falessi Cesare, " Semoventi italiani derivati dall'M13: una famiglia di poco noti veicoli da combattimento ", in "Storia Modellismo" number 3, year IV, March 1980.
- Pignato Nicola, "L'8 settembre a Parma ed il 433° carri M", in "Storia Modellismo" number 9, year II, September 1978.
- Pignato Nicola, "La "Difesa di Roma" - 1943", in "Storia Modellismo" number 9, year IV, September 1978.
- Prunetti Alberto, "1943 - La rivolta," in "Left," September 6, 2019.

## MAGAZINES

- "Il Carrista d'Italia," organ of the National Association of Italian Tankers, various issues.
- "Rivista," miscellaneous issues.
- "Storia Militare", miscellaneous issues.

## OTHER PUBLICATIONS

- AA.VV., "L'Esercito Italiano nella guerra di Liberazione", supplement to "Rivista Militare n°1, Stato Maggiore dell'Esercito - Ufficio Generale Promozione, Pubblicistica e Storia, Rome 2020.
- Graziano, "La vicenda di Silvio Gridelli, soldato aversano resistente a Porta San Paolo nel '43", in "La Resistenza nel Sud - Le azioni spontanee partigiane", acts of the International Congress of Caserta- Mignano Montelungo - San Pietro Infine- 21- 24 October 2004, Caserta, 2005.

# TITOLI GIÀ PUBBLICATI
# TITLES ALREADY PUBLISHING

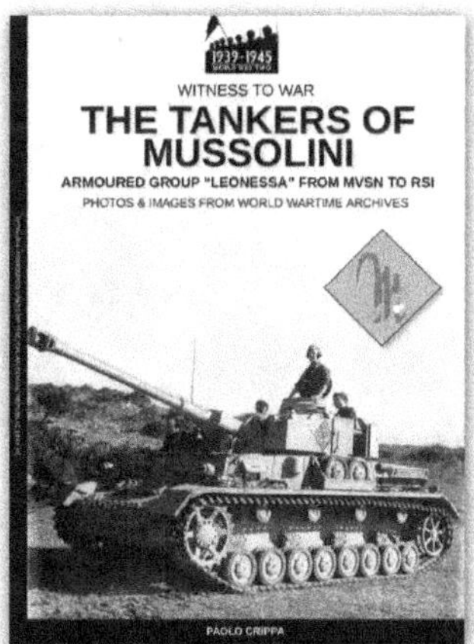

SOLDIERSHOP
PUBLISHING
BOOKS TO COLLECT

www.ingramcontent.com/pod-product-compliance
Lightning Source LLC
LaVergne TN
LVHW060346200726
843507LV00005B/987